# Putting Faith in Neighborhoods

# Putting Faith in Neighborhoods

## *Making Cities Work through Grassroots Citizenship*

STEPHEN GOLDSMITH

**with a case study by Ryan Streeter**

**Hudson Institute**

*Putting Faith in Neighborhoods*
*Making Cities Work through Grassroots Citizenship*
Stephen Goldsmith with a case study by Ryan Streeter
ISBN 1-55813-128-0
Copyright © 2002 Hudson Institute, Inc.

Printed in the United States of America.

For information about obtaining additional copies of this or other Hudson Institute
publications, contact:

Hudson Institute Publications
P.O. Box 1020
Noblesville, IN 46061
Toll free: 888-554-1325
Fax: 317-913-2392

Or, visit Hudson's online bookstore at http://www.hudson.org.

# Contents

### SECTION THREE
### The City and Citizenship Tomorrow

## CASE STUDY

# PREFACE

We are living in a time of great promise. Americans across the nation have responded to last year's horrific acts of terror not with the fear their enemies had predicted, but with compassion and patriotism. They have responded to insecurity by helping others feel secure. They have confronted hateful nihilism with kindness and hope.

The outpouring of compassion in the wake of last year's terrorist attacks helped us all remember who we are. We are not merely a nation of consumers and spectators but of neighbors and citizens. We measure the strength of our communities not by their tax base but by the commitment their residents have for each other. We understand citizenship to be more about our active contribution to the good of others than our passive enjoyment of rights.

We are witnessing a renewed interest in the importance of citizenship in America today. President George W. Bush's recent call to all Americans to help fight the war on terrorism by reaching out to others through acts of kindness hits on an important reality: the United States is only as strong as its communities, and its communities are only as strong as the citizens who comprise them. Large, important national goals such as homeland security are carried out through the vigilance and generosity of real people living in real towns, communities, and cities.

In his 2002 State of the Union address, President Bush asked Americans to help their communities and their country with two years of volunteer work during their lifetimes. He also called on significantly greater resources for the parent organization of AmeriCorps and Senior Corps, the Corporation for National and Community Service, which I am privileged to serve as chairman. Reactions to the proposal captured well the policy tensions present throughout the country and in this book. Liberals worried that volunteering would serve as an excuse for insufficient government action. Conservatives worried that expanded government funding to support the training and some expenses for volunteers would taint the recipient organizations.

When candidate Bush kicked off his presidential campaign in Indianapolis in 1999 with his moving and important "Armies of Compassion" speech, he called for a country that couples individual responsibility with the love of a caring neighbor. But, most important, he argued for a government that faces up to its responsibility to help those whom prosperity has left behind, by supporting, not supplanting, local individuals, institutions, and faith-based organizations. His view of government rejected both the idea that government alone could buy people out of poverty and that government could withdraw from its responsibilities.

Similarly, this book makes the point that citizenship cannot be achieved in the abstract or by a government agency bestowing rights on individuals or money on a problem, but by the responsibility people take for their neighborhoods. Citizenship begins at home and in the communities where we live. Social pathologies are best confronted not by large programs administered by professionals, but by citizens actively engaged in making their communities safer, healthier, more compassionate, and more productive. Government's role is to support these citizens and help them succeed.

As mayor of Indianapolis, I learned that no matter how good an idea might be or how well-crafted a policy, it would be merely an academic exercise if the city's residents were not involved in making it a reality. I saw firsthand that urban renewal begins with people helping people and claiming responsibility for the future of their neighborhoods. In the chapters that follow, I explain how Indianapolis served as a laboratory of citizenship. My hope is that this book will encourage others around the nation to begin building communities of citizens right where they live.

The book's title, *Putting Faith in Neighborhoods*, is a slogan for our times. To the extent that we can have faith in the generosity of one neighbor toward the next, American democracy will be strong. And to the extent that we can welcome to the table community-based organizations motivated by religious faith and sound values when we are trying to solve problems in our communities, we will be the better for it. For the past couple of decades, more and more people have agreed that putting faith in our neighborhoods is a wiser choice for the United States than putting faith in top-down solutions.

Today, because of the uniqueness of our times, this agreement is converting itself into a robust range of activity. The Corporation for National and Community Service is joining thousands of organizations in responding to President Bush's call for increased levels of community service. Faith-based organizations across the nation are asking, "How can our sacred mission serve public purposes?" Local and state public officials are figuring out how to involve grassroots organizations in the public effort to improve their communities. Federal agencies are aggressively engaged in making their programs more community-friendly by reaching out to traditionally excluded faith-based and neighborhood organizations. By putting faith in our neighborhoods, we are jointly beginning a new chapter in the history of American citizenship.

Aggressive government action, whether at the federal level or the local level described in this book, raises the apparent incongruity that is often the subject of conservatives' concern: Why is a mayor or a president so active in these issues if indeed the future of vibrant neighborhoods depends first and foremost on the private individual and communal efforts of neighbors? Certainly, the history of big government shows how it can suffocate local efforts, displace indigenous leadership, and reward bad behavior. This activity has also left many urban neighborhoods without the assets, personal and economic, that they need to move forward. The high taxes, bad infrastructure, and struggling schools in many of these neighborhoods have driven out middle-class parents, strong leaders, and the tax base. But in almost every one of these same areas, there are wonderful people committed to a common good, and great assets, such as churches, which are struggling to reach out to others.

Hence the fundamental issue in this book is how these sectors relate: How does a government executive use his or her authority and resources to nurture civil society? I faced this issue recently when President Bush announced, in his State of the Union address, his goal that every American should volunteer two years and that the Corporation for National and Community Service should be expanded greatly to provide more Senior Corps and AmeriCorps volunteers. How does government expansion support, rather than supplant, local leadership? With AmeriCorps, we are attempting as we did in Indianapolis, to reposition government as an agent that demands accountability while actively respecting community and faith-based organizations. Compassionate conservatism requires more local and state control and easier access to government by community and faith-based groups. President Bush's administration intends to make greater use of AmeriCorps for strengthening the administrative, financial, and technological capacities of grassroots change-makers. Investment of this sort strengthens the armies of compassion not by making them government's servant but by equipping them to do more of the good they already do.

My debts in writing this book extend beyond the process of authorship to the citizens of Indianapolis and the people in city hall that made the book possible. Courageous community activists such as Olgen Williams have clearly shown what citizenship on the ground should look like and have served as inspiration to many others. Many in city hall helped me push these initiatives forward, such as Bill Stanczykiewicz, the first director of the Front Porch Alliance, who had the vision and determination to turn ideas in city hall into active outreach to faith-based and community groups.

I have benefited greatly from my associations with many national and local leaders, including neighborhood advocate Robert Woodson Sr. and John DiIulio, the first director of the White House Office of Faith-Based and Community Initiatives, whose thoughtful and sincere hands-on approach in Philadelphia serves as a national model. The Annie E. Casey Foundation generously invested in our efforts. Ryan Streeter, Herb London, and their team of researchers at Hudson Institute took on this project and helped guide its successful completion.

Working to inspire neighborhood development, and writing about it, requires family sacrifices, and the support of my wife Margaret and my children has been consistent and inspiring.

# SECTION ONE
# The Three "C's":
# Citizen, City, Civil Society

# Chapter One

# Putting Citizens First

## A Crisis of Citizenship

The United States suffers from a crisis of citizenship. There are too many reasons—and some good ones—for people to feel so disconnected from their community that they would not dream of wasting their time doing something good for it. The state of America's cities exemplifies this crisis, and this book examines citizenship in the city as a means of identifying solutions to the national problem. The book flows out of the strategy we used during my tenure as mayor of Indianapolis in the 1990s to give residents in our distressed communities a greater say in their neighborhoods and greater control over their future. Some of our efforts worked well. Some did not. But we never wavered from the fundamental conviction that the residents of our city needed to become citizens again; they needed to be actively involved in crafting solutions to problems and creating the future of the city alongside the public officials whose job (at least in theory) is to serve them.

In particular we set out to foster "municipal citizenship." Municipal citizens are engaged in the community where they live. They have a personal stake in the public square. Local, municipal problems—whether they concern public safety or economic opportunity or housing availability—are "public square issues." That is, they usually cannot be confronted by government alone, nonprofit organizations alone, or business alone, but by each joined in a common effort. Municipal citizens work with government, grassroots organizations, faith-based organizations, and businesses to address concerns that everyone shares. Municipal citizenship requires public officials to be custodians, not controllers, of the public square, and it asks citizens to take on greater responsibility for their communities. Our empowerment efforts in Indianapolis were an attempt to restore the citizen to his rightful place in the city—with the hope of restoring higher levels of civility in the process.

The late University of Chicago sociologist Edward Shils has written, "In civility lies the difference between a well-ordered and disordered liberal democracy."[1] Civility is the virtue that makes civil society—that collection of voluntary associations, neighborhood groups, and other nongovernmental institutions such as congregations and families—work. And a strong civil society sets the foundation for effective markets, economic opportunity, and a genuine sense of empowerment and community—something that was lacking in many of my city's neighborhoods.

Within a month of my election as mayor in 1991, for example, two arson investigators were shot while on a stakeout near a public housing complex that was known for heavy drug activity, high crime, and other serious problems. No witnesses came forward with leads, and information was very tough to come by. More problematic was the way that residents appeared to accept such criminal behavior as the norm, rather than the exception. No neighborhood leaders marched on city hall demanding an end to the burning and shooting and doping. A sense of civic hopelessness pervaded the neighborhood.

Every American city has entire subcommunities where residents have little confidence in government and little optimism about the future of their neighborhood. In large part the residents have long been disconnected from the local centers of power and decision-making and have grown disaffected or even cynical. Overcoming this barrier to civic engagement, we thought, was critical to building a healthy civil society. If we failed in this, no amount of money targeted at crime or concentrated poverty would succeed in the long run.

So we set out to restore the hardest hit and longest neglected urban areas, those beset with the greatest problems and known for relatively high levels of socially destructive conduct. Our goal was to recreate a sense of civil society. But we knew that any attempt to strengthen the institutions of civil society would have to actively involve—and be driven by—the citizens themselves. As government, we had a responsibility to help citizens see what was possible for them to accomplish, support them in their efforts, and do whatever else was necessary to help them take back their communities from the forces that had made hopelessness a way of life.

Our modus operandi was to ask ourselves how government could be forceful, but respectful, and not usurp local leadership. Thus, we began an intense effort to motivate, nurture, train, recruit, and develop local leadership. We literally took it to the streets, going from neighborhood to neighborhood recruiting leaders and motivating residents who might want to gain control and authority over their neighborhoods to get involved. We wanted to help them become citizens again, not merely residents who paid too much in taxes and received (often inadequate) services.

To finance our efforts, we worked to make city government in general more efficient and effective. By outsourcing a large range of services, and by requiring that all city agencies meet specified performance levels, we were able to save hundreds of millions of dollars. We then used the savings to invest more in our neediest neighborhoods. In fact, we likely invested more in the neighborhoods than had been invested in them since World War II altogether.

Interestingly, we received accolades early on for our efforts to create a culture of performance within city government—something that we considered a means, not an end, of good governance. To be sure, our efforts to contract out services that government agencies had previously provided freed up significant resources to invest in neighborhoods. But saving money was the easy part. Investing it in a way to leverage permanent increases in "social capital" was much more difficult.

Much has been written about the importance of social capital and the need for a strong civil society. Less, in my opinion, has been written about how social capital can be increased in actual, concrete ways, or more specifically, how municipal citizenship can be effectively cultivated. This book chronicles how we set out to nurture municipal citizenship and stronger neighborhoods in Indianapolis, including our particular emphasis on the role of faith-based organizations.

## The Challenge of Citizenship

Although I had inherited a city with relatively low taxes, a good bond rating, and an overall healthy economy, Indianapolis, like most other large American cities, had steadily lost businesses and workers to the suburbs. From my office on the twenty-fifth floor of the city-county building, I could look to the horizon and see high-rise office buildings glistening on the north side of town—titans of the suburbs, where wealth, jobs, and better schools had relocated in the past three decades.

Meanwhile, the urban neighborhoods beneath my office, which stretched out in concentric circles to the suburbs, had become much less vital, less safe, and less neighborly. Those who could not afford to move out were left behind to dwell in the midst of high crime, poor services, and shrunken job markets.

Beginning in the 1960s and continuing for more than thirty years, the Great Society poured more than $5.5 trillion into programs that were allegedly designed to fight poverty. During that time, big government systems such as welfare created an attitude of entitlement among those in need and marginalized the local, faith-based and other community groups that often are highly effective in transforming individuals' lives. Indeed, America's value-generating civic institutions were often derided as oppressive, parochial backwaters of bigotry and ignorance.

Yet even with the high level of government spending, social problems only worsened. From the 1960s to the 1990s, violent crime in the United States rose more than 450 percent. The divorce rate rose from 16 to 40 percent of all marriages. The percentage of babies born out of wedlock rose from 5.3 percent to 29.5 percent. Fatherlessness rose from 17.5 percent to 38 percent of all children, reaching 90 percent in some urban neighborhoods.[2] For children growing up in broken homes and communities, economic opportunity remained as low as ever, and the likelihood of becoming a victim of crime as high as ever. Although recent statistics show some improvement in some of these areas, the totality of the harm remains enormous. At best, Great Society programs were relieving symptoms, rather than causes, of problems.

The breakdown of the family and the steep rise in criminal and antisocial behavior proved devastating to urban neighborhoods. I saw this firsthand while serving for twelve years as prosecutor in Indianapolis before becoming mayor. During that time I worked hard to ensure that those who engaged in antisocial and improper conduct paid the full legal consequences. Among other things, I prosecuted record numbers of individuals and held noncustodial parents responsible to their children and community.

But despite my belief in the importance of strongly enforcing the legal consequences of destructive behavior, my experience as prosecutor impressed on me the limits of law and authority without a properly functioning civil society. Unless attitudes, values, and habits change, few permanent benefits follow. Civil society, it turns out, depends as much on these factors as on the rule of law.

The question for government officials, of course, is what the proper role of government should be in a civil society. This question is not a new one. In the eighteenth century, for example, Adam Ferguson's *An Essay on the History of Civil Society* made the case that society is civil when commerce flourishes, local associations have real influence in their communities, and people are as demanding as they are humane in their expectations of themselves and others as citizens. This view of society, similar to the view that animated America's founders, posits a carefully balanced and nuanced role for government. If government tries to do too much, it often strips away the motivation people have to be engaged in their communities. If it does too little, citizens often do not have the resources or access to information to tackle their problems. But when government provides help in a way that stimulates and reinforces self-governance, then it truly works well. And in turn, when self-governance becomes a habit, the institutions of government are freed up to do fewer things, but to do them well.

In the thirty years leading up to the early 1990s, most urban areas experienced failure on both sides of the equation. As Harvard sociologist Robert Putnam expressed in his book *Bowling Alone*, America experienced a steep decline in "social capital" over the past three decades, with membership in civic-minded organizations dropping dramatically. "We kibitz," Putnam writes, "but we don't play. We maintain a façade of formal affiliation, but we rarely show up. We have invented new ways of expressing our demands that demand less of us. . . . We are less likely to turn out for collective deliberation. . . . We are less generous with our money. . . . More of our social connectedness is one shot, special purpose, and self-oriented."[3] Americans trust each other less than they used to. They have experienced a weakening of social ties, and they participate less in political, civic, and religious associations than they did thirty years ago. Even when they appear to be volunteering more, they do so as individuals and less in the context of community projects. In cities, these problems are exacerbated. Bureaucracies are created to reduce reliance on social capital. People lose incentive to engage in their communities. More problems result, order is tightened, and the problems spiral.

George Washington University professor Amitai Etzioni has noted that in the 1960s and after, "moral suasion as a foundation of social order" declined, and as traditional values fell out of fashion, they were never replaced by "any strong new shared values." Etzioni astutely points out that this was more than a move in the direction of freedom and autonomy: it was also a move toward anarchy. Anarchy, not autonomy, produces results like drastic rises in violence, numbers of prisoners, drug abuse, and teenage promiscuity.[4]

Indeed, rule-driven, top-down, one-size-fits-all bureaucracies and programs are all but incapable of providing help for people in an individualized way. Instead, they are good at treating everyone equally, even when the treatment is not good. For example, a poor working mother may be prevented from improving her situation because of a lack of transportation, child care, education, training, or perhaps because of family violence or the absence of her children's father. For each of those problems there is a distinct bureaucracy for her to deal with, and seldom (if ever) is the assistance coordinated or tailored to her needs.

By contrast, small, local, civic associations and religious organizations have the detailed knowledge and flexibility necessary to administer the right combination of loving compassion and rigorous discipline appropriate for each citizen. Similarly, those same organizations rather than government are the most effective at fostering citizenship, nurturing families, and encouraging civic pride.

They are the most effective at dealing with what Harvard political and social theorist Michael Sandel has identified as one of the greatest challenges of our times: reversing a pervasive sense that our most important civic institutions are unraveling and a feeling that we are not in control of the forces that have the greatest effect on our lives.[5] We saw that this feeling was especially strong in the neighborhoods that were in the worst conditions. So our challenge (and the continuing challenge for most governments) was *to foster—but not to control—*the kind of environment in which communities successfully attacked the core causes of problems at the ground level.

In order to make this practical, I drew on the work of Robert Woodson of the National Center for Neighborhood Enterprise, who emphasizes the value of grassroots leadership, and the writing of Northwestern University's John McKnight, who emphasizes that community development should build on a neighborhood's assets rather than its problems. I asked our planning department to create a map for me that charted the most significant stabilizing organizations in our neighborhoods, whether they were for-profit, faith-based, or nonprofit. Other than the under-recognized presence of small businesses, the most frequently cited organizations on the map were churches and, to a lesser degree, neighborhood associations or community-development corporations. These are some of the fundamental institutions of civil society. To turn our distressed neighborhoods around, we made a conscious effort to foster the growth of these institutions in order to give residents a sense of being in control over their own future.

We were simply trying to respond to a problem that Robert Nisbet had called a "crisis" four decades earlier and which was a real difficulty—if not a crisis—for us. He wrote:

> Our present crisis lies in the fact that whereas the small traditional associations, founded upon kinship, faith, or locality, are still expected to communicate to individuals the principal moral ends and psychological gratifica-

tions of society, they have manifestly become detached from positions of functional relevance to the larger economic and political decisions of our society. Family, local community, church, and the whole network of informal interpersonal relationships have ceased to play a determining role in our institutions.[6]

Volumes of books and articles have been produced in the last twenty years detailing the decline of civic responsibility and the role of "the small traditional associations" in America. Much of this literature, however, has focused on "the principal moral ends and psychological gratifications of society" provided by these associations at the expense of Nisbet's main point—the need for those associations to have a direct influence on large, and especially government, institutions.

While we expected that our community-based organizations would help shape solid values ("principal moral ends") and provide a sense of community ("psychological gratifications"), our real challenge was to ensure that participation in these organizations would truly create changes in our larger, impersonal institutions. Many of the Indianapolis residents who felt helpless in their communities were members of organizations where values were reinforced and the sense of community was strong. But their helplessness came from the basic disconnection they were experiencing between their community institutions and the larger institutions of local government.

Community engagement for its own sake may well miss the point. We did not want to miss the point. We wanted to make sure that increased citizen participation in community affairs affected the way that government did its business, and resulted in improvements that citizens could really see.

Our approach to strengthening citizens and civil society was based on two fundamental principles:

- *Habits of self-governance and personal responsibility are at the heart of a healthy civil society and must be promoted in all efforts to combat social problems.*
- *The residents of a city are wise enough to provide direction to their neighborhoods, and government must be responsive to this wisdom.*

These principles essentially play off one another. The first acknowledges that citizens must do their part. They have to promote the habits of citizenship in their homes and neighborhoods in order for civil society to work. The second principle obligates public officials to do their part and reach out to the citizens with attentive ears. This requires not just an occasional town hall meeting but a fundamental shift in the way that most public administrations interface with the communities they serve. Both citizens and city have an obligation to do their part, to change their habits, to act on behalf of the common good.

When we began our efforts in Indianapolis in 1992, these principles ran against the conventional wisdom of academics, bureaucrats, and media professionals. They still do today in spite of the fact that many more policymakers are accustomed to "community-based solutions" than they were a decade ago. Our experience showed us that these principles are critical factors in building a better, stronger, and more vibrant civil society—one in which the vast majority of citizens have confidence in the future, share a commitment to a core set of values, take charge of their communities, and respect each other and each other's property.

### Personal Responsibility

Regarding the first principle, conventional wisdom for the past several decades has been silent on the role of personal responsibility as a condition for overcoming problems. Civil society crumbles when its citizens do not uphold high standards of behavior in their personal and public lives. The mantra of "value neutrality" so prevalent in many of our schools, media, and other important institutions does not result in neutral values. It results in having no way to combat dangerous—or downright bad—values.

I first noticed this fifteen years ago while actively involved in collecting child support as a prosecutor. Mothers on welfare were my primary clients, since they represented the largest population of poor women seeking child support. These moms were candid with me: they knew that if they went to work, they would lose not only welfare but many other benefits as well, and they rationally concluded that working harmed their families. The state had created dependency and undermined the very values it purported to champion.

Neighborhood involvement for its own sake, of course, is worthwhile. However, when a neighborhood-based mediating institution promotes values that align with those articulated through the democratic process, the results are self-enforcing. This is especially the case with religious organizations. When churches, mosques, and synagogues teach about the ills of teen pregnancy, they reinforce government's messages asserted through child-support enforcement and abstinence-education programs.

We committed substantial effort to discouraging teen pregnancies through various local government efforts, and we encouraged citywide involvement of religious organizations in this issue as well. It was obvious to me that the religious response would always carry more authority than my exhortations. I remember visiting Greenwood Community Church, a suburban congregation known for partnering with inner-city churches, and listening to Pastor Charles Lake preach a forceful, compelling sermon about the obligation that derives from God to take care of one's body and to bear children within the bond of marriage. His eloquent speech carried a moral force that was good for our community, regardless of one's opinions about his theology. Advocates of segregating religious speech from public discourse are never able to replace the moral and publicly beneficial value that comes from faith. Public officials would do well to make a practice of welcoming all expressions of sound values and healthy behavior within their communities.

Our empowerment effort set out explicitly to leverage a few core values that would seem to be necessary for a vibrant community, including respect for each other and their property: self-restraint, work, and civic duty. Government does not play the role of moral educator well, and we never pretended that it did. But it can stand behind those organizations and institutions that cultivate habits of self-governance and mutual obligation, and it can form policies that encourage good values—which is what we tried to do. Personal responsibility is not the only condition for overcoming social problems, but without it, all other attempts to eliminate causes of poverty, crime, and civic apathy do little good.

Take the example of fatherlessness. Not only had welfare-state policies created a culture that made it pay to be a single mother who continued to have out-of-wedlock children, but it rooted itself in a philosophy that said that fathers were of little consequence to children's well-being. When Barbara Dafoe Whitehead wrote her now-famous 1993 article, "Dan Quayle Was Right" in the *Atlantic Monthly*, which argued that the former vice president was justified in criticizing the fictional TV character, Murphy Brown, for choosing to have a child out of wedlock—public debate was fierce. Many people took offense at Whitehead's claims.

Nine years later, that issue of the *Atlantic Monthly* is the magazine's third best-selling issue in its 86-year history. More important, a consensus has emerged based on an impressive collection of research that says the best way to improve a child's chances of a good education and successful life is to reduce teen parenting and to enhance the chances that the child will grow up in a family with two, preferably married, parents. Children with two involved parents do better in school, suffer fewer psychological problems, and enjoy the promise of a better future. However important they may be, money and programs cannot replace the positive contribution that a responsible father makes in the lives of his children.

Individuals need to take responsibility for improving their lives and the lives of their children. Some people consider asking citizens to do their part and take responsibility as intolerable and presumptuous. I discovered, though, that successful neighborhood leaders are among the loudest advocates of responsible behavior.

In the last year of my tenure as mayor, the pastor of a religious shelter for the homeless in a tough part of town brought me an unusual complaint. His shelter, funded by private donations, required all who resided there to pray and work. The area around the shelter was clean, and its residents never loitered or posed a threat to nearby businesses and residences. A publicly funded shelter located next to him, which provided food but without the piety or the toil, consistently applied a downward pressure on the surrounding neighborhood. Its residents hung out on the streets, occasionally wandered into the pastor's facilities smelling of alcohol, and made area business owners uncomfortable. The pastor was frustrated because the other shelter's food-without-responsibility approach to assistance would sometimes lure the people he served to take the easier road. They would fall back into the lives he was trying to help them escape, and the cycle of despair would continue. For this community leader, who lived in the same neighborhood as the people he served, neglecting responsibility was directly related to the despair he witnessed all around him every day. This pastor, like the thousands of community builders around the country who truly care about rehabilitating lives and improving neighborhoods, believed that personal responsibility is a necessary part of the equation.

### Putting Official "Faith" in Citizenship

If the first principle places a burden of responsibility on citizens, the second places responsibility on public officials whose everyday decisions affect citizens' lives. Through their choices about programs and policies, too many bureaucrats and elected officials affect the lives of ordinary people without ever consulting them. Perversely, many of these decisions hurt rather than help poor families over time.

In our cities, many people have to live with "solutions" to their problems that they never would have selected had they been given a choice. Aside from being fundamentally undemocratic, these centralized policies make people dependent on government without helping them stand on their own feet and enjoy the freedom necessary to give their kids the kinds of homes, schools, and neighborhoods they want. In this sense, government undermines responsibility and creates an entitlement mentality.

In many instances, professional public managers make very important decisions affecting neighborhoods because even neighborhood residents generally presume that these professionals know best. The details
of the decisions, so the presumption goes, are too dense and complicated
for residents. Well-trained planners in our Department of Metropolitan
Development frequently made land-use decisions and imposed rules for
signs and development in a manner they absolutely believed to be in a
neighborhood's long-term interest and better than anything residents
could manage on their own. They preferred to work without intervention by the community development corporations (CDCs), who often
employed consensus decision-making, and small neighborhood groups
who complicated things. The results of their actions, however, often frustrated residents, who with each such occurrence were less inclined than
before to invest time in their neighborhood.

Hoover Institution fellow Thomas Sowell has analyzed the way that
political decision-making in America has evolved toward a domain of
specialists disconnected from the interests and concerns of everyday
people:

> [W]ithin democratic nations, the locus of decision mak-
> ing has drifted away from the individual, the family, and
> voluntary associations of various sorts, and toward gov-
> ernment. And within government, it has moved away
> from elected officials subject to voter feedback, and
> toward more insulated governmental institutions, such
> as bureaucracies and the appointed judiciary. These
> trends have grave implications, not only for individual
> freedom, but also for the social ways in which knowl-
> edge is used, distorted, or made ineffective.[7]

Participation in public decision-making gives citizens an important
stake in their communities. Residents usually know what is best for
them. When public managers ignore this, their actions and the compla-
cency of the residents become mutually reinforcing forces in a downward spiral. As professionals control too much decision making, citizens
become less invested and franchised, which accelerates further disin-
vestments and outmigration, which in turn causes even more top-down
decision making.

Too much government intervention leads to the distrust that comes
from what columnist Robert Samuelson has called "overpromising":

> What comes after entitlement is, or ought to be, respon-
> sibility. It ought to be the animating ideal of public con-

duct and private behavior. We need to curb our casual use of government—especially, the federal government—as the problem solver of last resort. It has clearly failed in this role, and unless we narrow its responsibilities, we can expect failure to continue and worsen. We need to recognize that society can be strong only if its many constituent parts—families, private businesses, community, religious, and professional organizations, as well as government—are strong. Rhetorically at least, the transformation has already occurred. Politicians of both parties now routinely invoke "personal responsibility," "leaner government," or "reinvented government." But responsibility is behavior, not rhetoric, and politicians proclaim it more than they practice it. . . . Unfortunately, this behavior—overpromising, as I have put it—now dominates our political culture.[8]

The best way to keep from overpromising is to engage citizens in the construction of policies—the things you are promising—and to ask them to make a promise in return for each of the promises you make to them. In other words if public officials and citizens work together to build policy and implement programs, then no one can fairly blame the other if things do not work out well.

In order to do this, citizens need to be with public officials *during*—not after—the preparation of plans and proposals. Citizens know where the trouble spots are in their neighborhoods. Different kinds of troubles require different kinds of solutions, and each neighborhood is different. What this means for public officials is that a universally applied, centrally administered policy may not help anyone. Many of our public institutions are built for an entitlement culture in which government's job is to collect information and resources, reassemble them according to rigidly determined formulas, and then redistribute them to the people and groups it has decided need them. We need more effective and accountable institutions that put people, not bureaucracy, first.

### *The Right Balance: The Example of Policing*

Public services and citizen empowerment can, however, complement each other. Policing provides a case in point. Older, rapid-response policing methods used power and force to create safety. In high-crime neighborhoods, before the initiatives described in this book were implemented, neighbors would obey a direct police order, but most of them neither respected nor aided the police. They never viewed the production of safety as their responsibility or as something they could affect. But the movement toward community policing strategies, no matter how difficult and spotty in their initial success, provided an opportunity to make changes.

On this point, I am reminded of two very different Indianapolis neighborhoods facing a similar problem: crack cocaine, which came late to Indianapolis and was a major problem after I became mayor. All districts and areas of the city were ordered to commence the transition to community policing immediately. One of the neighborhoods included a section where the residents were involved in our empowerment initiatives. The other, on the east side, was not. On the east side many of the officers continued to view many residents in their high-crime areas as problems to be controlled. And the residents viewed order as a problem they expected the police to solve. Their fear and lack of involvement actually created an unhealthy dependence on the police, which neither side recognized as such but simply accepted as normal.

A few miles from this hot spot, the other neighborhood produced a strikingly different result. We involved neighborhood leaders, pastors, residents, and local business people in the process of designing ways to fight successfully the crack crisis and all the other problems it generates. The neighbors accepted training for cellular crime-watch reporting programs, and then began organizing antidrug marches. They began actively sending in tips about narcotic dealers. Police in return worked with neighborhood leaders to intensify street-level policing in the areas the residents nominated. They put officers on foot and bikes, and had them frequently visit schools and youth programs. In a neighborhood implementing similar reforms, the police even handed out "Indianapolis Police Department Trading Cards" so that young people could get to know them by name.

Once this activity begins, it generates positive second-order effects as citizens begin to see what their action can produce. At a meeting with pastors in the more successful neighborhood, Reverend Roosevelt Sanders of Mt. Vernon Missionary Baptist Church came forward to share his vision for a faith-based drug relapse prevention facility in the neighborhood. Reverend Sanders understood that if drug-dependent individuals were to overcome their addiction, counseling needed to be at least as accessible as the drugs. By offering professional and pastoral help within the neighborhood, the facility would provide a healthy alternative to residents tempted by drugs and crime, while sending a clear message that the church and its members were taking back their neighborhood. Previously, people in the neighborhood would have to go across the city for drug treatment. Now they would have a caring faith community to help them kick a bad habit before it restarted.

He worked with city hall to acquire a vacant property at an intersection that used to be a haven of drugs and crime. Now it is a beacon of hope in a neighborhood that has revitalized itself so quickly that people have flocked from all around the country to see what real life-and-blood empowerment looks like.

Another neighborhood took note of these successes and decided to make public safety a citizen-driven project in its part of town as well. They committed a lot of time to building solid relationships with the officers and created the Old National Road Business Coalition, a group of local business owners, pastors, and nonprofit organization directors who met regularly to design safety and community renewal initiatives. They began working with the Front Porch Alliance, our broad-based effort to support the work of Indianapolis's faith-based and other community-redeeming organizations, which I will treat at greater length in Chapters Four and Seven. The Front Porch Alliance worked with a very enterprising pastor, Jay Height, to recruit 60 local businesses along downtown's East Washington Street (formerly National Road) to partner with Height's Shepherd Community Center to address crime and neighborhood revitalization issues.

One of the first challenges the Coalition confronted was a crime-infested alley across the street from Shepherd. Drug dealers would sell on this historic corridor and then escape through the alley, which was too narrow for police car pursuit. The Coalition called the Front Porch Alliance with a proposal to close the alley and build in its place a community garden. The Alliance cut through the red tape of more than fifty nearby businesses and city agencies to get all the necessary permits and paperwork to close the alley, and then it arranged for public-works employees to jackhammer the cement and clear away the debris. The alley soon disappeared and was replaced by a small park and a couple rows of trees. The drug dealers disappeared because the advantages of doing business in the alley disappeared. Only three months later, crime was down 13.5 percent in the blocks surrounding the newly built park.

These efforts at reducing crime and improving life were not the product of a crime strategy concocted behind closed doors at city hall. The residents of the neighborhood were involved from the beginning. The community policing efforts took on a disposition unique to the neighborhood, and the pastors knew they could make demands of city hall to help them. Shutting down crack houses is not easy. Without the support of city hall, they probably would not have succeeded on their own. However, they were able to ask us to help them. We knew that for them to be free to build a neighborhood their children could be proud of, we needed to let them lead us to the solution. We needed to let them be free to resist our ideas for their neighborhoods if they thought their ideas were better.

## A City Where Citizenship Matters: The Indigenous Institutional Glue

In addition to family, educational, and religious influences, the key ingredient to successfully applying the two principles previously named—responsibility and citizen participation—is an active culture of community-based institutions. In fact, the two principles operate together harmoniously when neighborhood-level groups are busy enlisting volunteers, working with city officials, reaching out to other community-based organizations, building relationships with funders, and so on. Municipal citizenship flourishes in a rich culture of value-enhancing relationships, networks, and organizations.

*Local leadership within organizations that have a reputation of concern for the community can create an environment in which responsibility can be encouraged.* Pastors knock on doors asking residents why they were not at the neighborhood cleanup day the last Saturday, which enforces norms of responsibility. Community centers watch juvenile crime rates go down because of their after-school programs, encouraging residents to keep up the good work. Residents enjoy a newly rehabilitated park, the recent improvement of which resulted from residents petitioning city officials through their neighborhood association, which reinforces the virtues of organizing and cooperating. Mentors at the community center down the street learn that sacrificing time pays off when they see the children they mentored awarded at a ceremony for academic excellence. In these and similar instances the habits of citizenship are learned, promoted, and developed.

Citizens engage themselves in their communities when they truly have a stake in the future of an area and know that their actions matter. And when they know that their actions matter, they exercise the habits of self-government such as self-restraint, volunteerism, compassion, and hard work. They demand higher standards of themselves, their neighbors, and their public officials. This circumstance requires reciprocity: action from the city, a reason for citizens to care (such as homeownership), and a mechanism for them to express themselves.

*Neighborhood associations create an organizational structure with which government can work.* Organizations can sustain change, receive grants, build partnerships; individuals usually cannot. In addition, while interest groups tend to represent classes of people or professional groups, neighborhood associations provide a way to sustain change and focus interests on a real, concrete part of the city.

Articulate leaders of local groups, whether faith-based or secular, can communicate the needs of those who are poor to those who can help. Their organizations provide a structure capable of bringing available services closer to those who need them. Local associations also enable a group of people to make their collective interests known to elected officials and then help outline the implementation of certain policies and services. Peter Berger and Richard John Neuhaus wrote in *To Empower People* that mediating structures such as neighborhood, family, church, and voluntary associations should occupy a more central place in democratic processes. Their basic claims were that "mediating structures are essential for a vital democratic society," that "public policy should protect and foster" them, and that public policy should, wherever possible, utilize them "for the realization of social purposes."[9]

Both of these essential association functions make active citizenship more likely and more appealing. They safeguard against initiatives that get designed but never fully implemented. They are the promise of improvement in a city.

In hard-pressed city neighborhoods, however, citizenship does not come easily. Government usurpation of good works, coupled with fear and a lack of stability on the streets, produces little incentive for civic engagement. For example, as we redeveloped inner-city neighborhoods, we frequently rallied residents and corporate volunteers to participate in beautification and cleanup activities.

One Saturday, several mayor's office employees joined with community leaders in cleaning up an alley littered with trash, mattresses, and illegal dumping. Somewhat expectedly, only a handful of neighbors joined our small band as it ventured down the alley. What most surprised me, however, was how few people came out their back doors to watch the cleanup as it passed their houses. When I encouraged one man to join us, he stared blankly and returned inside.

Even if government reduces its monopoly over good deeds, citizens are unlikely to start simply serving the public square on their own. Government needs to reach out to mediating neighborhood organizations by supporting volunteer training, nurturing leadership, making positive investments in effective programs, sending supportive signals to the community, and involving them in decision-making. When government does these things, participation in associations increases. Participation, in turn, not only produces individual commitment, but it also strengthens the positive effect of the mediating institution itself.

The reason Robert Putnam's *Bowling Alone* has attracted so much attention in recent years is because people associate participation in civic associations with overall civic health. Putnam's thesis that Americans are less involved in community projects and local associations than they used to be suggests to us that something very important about who we are is at risk. His provocative claim led scholars to disagree about the extent of the decline in social capital in America, but almost everyone agrees that declining civic engagement itself hurts democratic institutions.[10] This is because local associations are incubators of virtue, public debate, the art of negotiation, and compassionate outreach to those in need. Without these, a democracy grows weak.

John McKnight has popularized the term "community assets" as a way to talk about local organizations that do socially important work in a community at the grassroots level. A nonprofit local youth center that provides opportunities for children to develop academic and personal capabilities does not enlarge the tax base or create many jobs, but it is an asset because it invests in kids by giving them attention and something constructive to do with their time. It is a place where volunteers give of their time, and in general, it makes the community a better place. Focusing on assets places priorities on building what is good, not simply on getting rid of what is bad.

Community assets also tend to promote what the French philosopher Jean-Jacques Rousseau called active, rather than passive, citizens. A passive citizen, he said, is a member of the State. An active citizen is a participant in a city or republic. It is interesting that he differentiated the political regime based on the kind of citizenship it promoted. The active citizen is engaged in making the community a better place and the passive citizen is content obeying laws and receiving services. We are all, in reality, active citizens at some points, passive at others. Our goal, though, should be to find ways to encourage each other to assume greater shares of active, or responsible, citizenship.

Management theorist Peter Drucker writes of the importance of the third sector of society—that "space" in which socially redeeming activity occurs between the institutions of government and market: "In the political culture of mainstream society individuals, no matter how well educated, how successful, how achieving, or how wealthy, can only vote and pay taxes. They can only react; they can only be passive. In the counterculture of the third sector, they are active citizens. This may be the most important contribution of the third sector."[11]

While Rousseau never inspired much of an interest among his followers in local associations as the way to cultivate active citizenship (quite the opposite), Drucker's third sector, to be effective, presupposes them. Without a vibrant culture of citizen-driven associations, the active citizen would be left alone to cast an occasional vote and make a telephone call to a representative every now and then. In all probability, that citizen will eventually become passive.

Alexis de Toqueville famously marveled in the early nineteenth century at the manner in which Americans were "forever forming associations," whether they were distributing books, building schools, proclaiming truth, or constructing publicly significant buildings. "In every case, at the head of a great new undertaking, where in France you would find the government or in England some territorial magnate, in the United States you are sure to find an association."[12] Toqueville discovered a peculiarly American idea that the citizens themselves, through their associations, were chiefly responsible for the creation of the public good.

We simply knew that we could not empower the people of Indianapolis without empowering local associations, neighborhood groups, and faith-based organizations. Robert Nisbet called these social groups mediating, or intermediate, associations because they stand between the individual and the larger, more impersonal institutions of government. The most significant social problems, he said, were met "however inadequately at times, through the associated means of these social groups."[13]

Instead of taking the moralistic approach to self-governance that told people to become organized, behave themselves, and start acting like citizens, we reached out to neighborhoods. Soon after I was elected, we launched a citywide initiative called "Vision Indianapolis," in which scores of city officials went from neighborhood to neighborhood to meet with communities and help plan a future we all wanted to have. Our message was "organize yourselves and make demands on us—picket us if you have to, but be prepared to uphold your end of the bargain, and we'll uphold ours." We maintained this posture throughout my eight-year tenure. We employed the same strategy when we formed the Front Porch Alliance, which specifically reached out to faith-based organizations and other small grassroots groups. This strategy was rooted in the idea that if neighborhood groups became active, so would the citizens. Asked to organize themselves, residents began forming associations to tackle all sorts of problems.

The number of registered neighborhood associations doubled while I was in office. This prompted Michael Grunwald, in a critical article titled, "The Myth of the Supermayor," to write, "touchy-feely as it sounds, that may be [Goldsmith's] most lasting achievement. Police solve more crimes when residents will tell them what's going on. Kids learn more when their parents get involved in their schools. Neighborhoods improve when people stop sitting around and do something about them."[14] Though I disagreed with much of the article's criticism (and I never wanted to be a myth anyway), if this is my greatest accomplishment, then Indianapolis will be the better for it.

# Government Transition:
# From Professionalism to Partnership

Much has been written about changing the way that government and citizens relate to each other. Much has been written on the importance of the institutions of civil society such as voluntary and neighborhood associations. But converting the writing into changed practices is another matter. The "reinventing government" movement, for instance, has often focused too narrowly on enhanced customer service as the basic model of improved relations. Customer service is important, and we made it a central theme in many of our reforms because taxpayers need to have the same responsiveness as they would expect when they are shopping, banking, or buying a house. But if we do not look beyond customer service as a model, then we do not really ever get past the notion of the passive citizen who receives (often subpar) services.

A healthy interface between government and active, local associations requires a behavior change on the part of public officials. It requires a fundamental change in perspective since it often involves more effort, the appearance of less efficiency, and an occasional decision that looks "unprofessional." Professional mid-level managers are trained to apply their skills to solve problems. During my terms as mayor, the police might be fashioning a war on drugs, park planners designing a new park, and planners arriving at the right zoning decisions through their own internal processes—all at the same time. And this was all happening because of promises I had made to the public or because we were responding to complicated complaints from Indianapolis residents. Including neighborhood leaders in these kinds of processes without slowing things down is difficult. It is a challenge to involve citizens in a way that mediates between differing views and results in effective, practical solutions—especially if indigenous participation is to be real and not after-the-fact window dressing.

If we truly want to narrow the gap between the citizen and the public official who makes policy decisions, we need to understand municipal citizenship.

Residents become municipal citizens when they begin engaging themselves in their communities, serving public purposes, and collaborating with other stakeholders in the public square such as local government and community-serving nonprofits. In particular, three basic types of engagement contribute to the making of the municipal citizen.

*Pragmatic*

> *Solution-focused:* Citizens engage in their communities to take on a concrete problem.

> *Interest-based:* Basic, everyday concerns motivate citizens' engagement.

## Social Capital

> *Relationship-focused:* Citizens engage in their communities to build networks with others, to create symbiotic partnerships in which each member is stronger as a result of the partnership.
> *Asset-based:* Citizen engagement is driven primarily by existing relationships between people and organizations and a desire to expand, multiply, reinforce, and strengthen these relationships.

## Values-Enhancing

> *Responsibility-focused:* Citizens engage in their communities to reinforce values in individuals and institutions such as self-worth, self-sufficiency, a sense of purpose, mutual respect, productivity, and overall responsible behavior.
> *Values-based:* Citizen engagement is motivated by a sincere commitment to religious beliefs or a set of distinct moral values, along with a desire to see those beliefs and values reinforced in the community as a result of engagement.

Any given civic initiative, program, or project may combine all three of these. A pragmatic partnership focused on picking up trash in a specific neighborhood might evolve into a values-enhancing partnership as community leaders begin to promote the effort through schools, congregations, and community-based organizations as a civic obligation and means to demonstrate neighborhood pride. The task for community leaders and public officials is to understand the needs and expectations of all members in a partnership so that, say, stronger social capital is not expected from a primarily pragmatic collaboration.

Efforts to increase civic engagement and empower citizens often rely primarily on pragmatic partnerships and social-capital-building efforts. Community organizing that seeks to achieve a specific policy outcome is interest-based and targeted at pragmatic objectives. A citywide collaboration of summer youth programs may have as its stated objective the enhancement of educational and vocational skills, but it is primarily a social capital partnership due to the bridge-building it carries out among community-serving organizations and leaders.

Value-enhancing partnerships are often thought of separately, as part of a different category. Churches, some private schools, families—these are the instruments of values and morals. However, it takes strong values to foster responsibility for one's community. It also takes values to cultivate "habits of democracy" such as mutual respect, sacrificing time for the community, petitioning public leaders, and taking charge of one's neighborhood. When partnerships and organizations reinforce and teach the values that result in responsibility and habits of democracy, they are making a publicly important contribution. For this reason, it is in the interest of public officials, leaders of nonprofits, and directors of foundations to encourage these kinds of partnerships. Value-enhancing partnerships do not only strengthen values of individual citizens; they call institutions to operate at a higher level. They demand high levels of trust and integrity from collaborating public agencies and expect nonprofit leaders not to invest in change rather than maintaining the status quo.

In Indianapolis, we encouraged citizens to practice all three types of engagement. There were problems in need of citizen solutions. There were organizations in need of relationships, networks, and expanded access to opportunities. And there were values that needed reinforcing in order to give hope and stability to fragile communities. When all three types of engagement are embodied and actively carried out, residents become municipal citizens.

## Endnotes

[1] Edward Shils, *The Virtue of Civility: Selected Essays on Liberalism, Tradition, and Civil Society* (Indianapolis: Liberty Fund, 1997), 320.

[2] *Just the Facts: A Summary of Recent Information on America's Children and Their Families* (Washington, D.C.: National Commission on Children, 1993), and *1996 Green Book*, Committee on Ways and Means, U.S. House of Representatives (Washington, D.C.: Government Printing Office).

[3] Robert Putnam, *Bowling Alone: The Collapse and Revival of American Community* (New York: Simon and Schuster, 2000), 183-84.

[4] Amitai Etzioni, *The New Golden Rule: Community and Morality in a Democratic Society* (New York: Basic Books, 1996), 69, 71-72.

[5] Michael Sandel, *Democracy's Discontent: America in Search of a Public Philosophy* (Cambridge: Harvard University Press, 1996), 3.

[6] Robert Nisbet, *The Quest for Community* (Oxford: Oxford University Press, 1971), 54.

[7] *Knowledge and Decisions* (New York: Basic Books, 1980, 1996), 164.

[8] Robert Samuelson, *The Good Life and its Discontents: The American Dream in the Age of Entitlement, 1945-1995* (New York: Random House Times Books, 1995), 218-19.

[9] Peter Berger and Richard John Neuhaus, *To Empower People: From State to Civil Society*, Twentieth Anniversary Edition, ed. Michael Novak (Washington D.C.: AEI Press, 1996), 162-63.

[10] Prior to *Bowling Alone*, cited earlier, the Putnam articles that prompted much public debate about social capital are, "Bowling Alone: America's Declining Social Capital," *Journal of Democracy* 6, no. 1 (1994): 65-78, and "The Strange Disappearance of Civic America," *The American Prospect* 24 (Winter 1996): 34-48.

[11] Peter Drucker, *The New Realities in Government and Politics/in Economics and Business/in Society and World View* (New York: Harper and Row, 1989), 9.

[12] Alexis de Toqueville, *Democracy in America*, trans. George Lawrence (New York: HarperCollins, 1988), 513.

[13] Nisbet, 54.

[14] Michael Grunwald, "The Myth of the Supermayor," *The American Prospect* (September-October 1998): 20.

# Chapter Two

# Hope of Empowerment

## What Kind of Empowerment?

Engaging citizens and neighborhood associations in city hall initiatives is the art of municipal citizenship. Troubled neighborhoods suffer from a shortage of authority and control for two main reasons. On the one hand, overextended government has claimed too much power for itself over neighborhood affairs, while on the other, neighborhoods, like muscles, atrophy when neglected and grow weaker over against a strong public administration. The first problem grows larger every day as public officials make one decision after another without consulting residents. The second problem results in a dearth of motivation and a lack of influence at the street level. The question is thus: how does government return proper authority to—how does it empower—neighborhoods and thereby start building the long-neglected civic muscle tissue?

The term *empowerment* is one of those words that has found usage in just about every corner in society. It appears in the titles of myriad books, articles, conferences, and seminars. While the word has sometimes been superficially used to talk about a variety of self-improvement tactics, it generally means, as the name implies, getting more power into the hands of people who are disenfranchised in some way. In particular the word has been used frequently in the public policy community to denote a way to provide help to distressed communities.

Shortly before I took office, the leadership of a transitional neighborhood summoned me to a meeting. They presented a study from Ball State University's department of architecture that proposed the redevelopment of an important intersection, Forty-Second Street and College Avenue. I thought this corner had enormous importance in stabilizing what had become a troubled neighborhood. A few decades earlier, I attended movies in the neighborhood as a young adult and lived nearby while working summers during law school. The intersection now stood virtually abandoned, threatening stable neighborhoods around it. It was a very visible sign that hope and progress no longer meant anything in the area.

The proposal suggested substantial public and private investment in the area, coupled with significant private sector involvement. The millions of dollars in investments would be focused close to the epicenter of the crack epidemic in the area, and thus raising the money and guaranteeing the necessary safety seemed remote at best. A major disturbance in the area a few years after the ambitious study was published, but before the development work was finished, turned the streets into a war zone and demonstrated how much work was needed to forge a real partnership. Yet, eight years later, three of the four corners at the intersection featured new investments. Crime—especially violent crime—had substantially decreased, and hope existed in the area for the first time in a while. This was an achievement not of increases in public and private spending, however, but of a neighborhood empowered to tackle crime head-on through a strong relationship with city hall, law enforcement, and business. Neighbors demanded, and then supported, stronger law enforcement, the formation of an advisory committee for the precinct, bike patrols, and an effective process whereby they could report crack houses.

We called our comprehensive approach to strengthening neighborhoods the Neighborhood Empowerment Initiative. Its goal was to end the long-standing tradition—found in almost any large city—of making neighborhoods dependent on city government and its programs, and begin a new tradition in which city hall acts as a supporter of the self-determination and enterprise resident in each neighborhood.

So what does "empowerment" mean, and how does it work? The public policy community so frequently uses the word to indicate help for troubled urban populations that it has come to have a variety of meanings. It is worth surveying a few of them and making clear what we meant by empowerment in Indianapolis.

## *Political Activist Empowerment*

The basic tenet of this model is that the capture of political power is equal to empowerment. In his book, *The Politics of Empowerment*, which chronicles how widely the concept of empowerment is used today, political science professor Robert Weissberg describes our kind of empowerment this way: "Empowerment means coercing reluctant officials into bestowing benefits under their decree or capturing command centers outright."[1] Progressive politics in the early twentieth century set the stage for this kind of empowerment in which well-funded national groups seek direct political influence in Washington. As Weissberg notes, however, what drives movements such as these is "the unexpressed belief that *only* government—principally Washington—can supply sought ends," and he skeptically adds, "That political action is the wellspring of progress is, of course, arguable."[2]

Of course, national special-interest efforts affect local redevelopment when the national organizations representing CDCs or public housing lobby for authority. Sometimes these efforts complement local efforts, as when community-development interest groups lobby for tax credits that help create a stronger market for low-income housing providers. At other times, the national groups interfere, such as when public-housing authorities lobbied Congress to prevent home, or local, rule, and insisted instead that the Department of Housing and Urban Development protect its nationally driven and centralized way of doing business.

Whatever the case may be, empowerment considered solely as the capture of political power is simply too one-sided, even when positive things result. Interest has always been at the heart of politics, and it always will be. But empowerment focused only on capturing political centers of power only really empowers people to more effectively get what they want—and what people want is often only a short-term fix. Empowerment also has to equip people to engage in the kinds of practices and join in the kinds of partnerships that produce long-lasting change.

## *"Toquevillian" Empowerment*

What I call Toquevillian empowerment is that kind of grassroots control that citizens exercise over what happens in their community and that the French journalist Alexis de Toqueville so greatly admired when he visited America in the 1830s. It insists strongly in the decentralization of core services to citizen control. It holds that choices affecting citizens' lives need to be handed over to the authority of citizens and the mediating institutions they inhabit. To this end, it contends that empowering value-shaping organizations, families, neighborhood associations, and faith-based organizations helps translate their values into action. When this is successfully accomplished, problems in those residents' communities begin to diminish and overall quality of life is improved.

This form of empowerment closely, but not completely, resembles what we attempted to carry out in Indianapolis. It was never our contention that citizen groups control every decision, nor that they be burdened with all imaginable service provision minutia. Citizens may not want or be prepared to undertake control of everything going on such as trash pickup, selection of companies to repair their roads, and so on. They neither may want nor be prepared to decide how the Local Department of Health should allocate all of its funds. What is most important is that they have the opportunity to give their input and know that public officials will listen when they speak.

Also, more citizen participation will not necessarily result in overall improved conditions. Without good information and timely assistance from government, residents of a community might only have their weariness to show for their efforts, while their streets might still be filthy, home to stray dogs, and unsafe for their children to cross. It is easy to grow nostalgic about the voluntary organizations of the past, but we cannot hoist expectations on today's community-based organizations that they are not equipped to fulfill.

Any empowerment effort needs to take the Toquevillian element seriously, however. Weissberg, describing empowerment that seeks to make use of local mediating structures, writes, "It rests on proven methods—the task is to extend what is already there, not invent novelties."[3] Families and community and faith-based organizations are already there. They are already at work in their communities, acting without regard to reward but with a concern for the citizens right in their midst. Without them, any empowerment effort is defeated at the start.

### Economic Empowerment

Money is important. But it is not the first priority in starting an empowerment effort. Simply getting money into the hands of people disenfranchised from the economic mainstream has rarely proved effective on its own. Any public resources will always seem in too short supply to meet the demand, even in an age of surpluses. No matter how much funding is given to a government-sponsored activity, the administrators of that activity will likely say they need more money to be effective—particularly when the activity is addressing issues related to urban decay, crime, joblessness, and broken families.

A new consensus holds that financial stability and a sense of self-worth are based on the habits, practices, and ways of life that promote work and enterprise. Welfare reform set the stage for economic liberty by freeing individuals from dependency and counterproductive incentives. But most people now agree that working poor families will only escape poverty if they, first, stay employed and, second, develop a vocational path. This requires connecting workforce-development initiatives to the community's larger economic development plans. People cannot improve their job skills and develop vocations in a vacuum; they need to be connected to employment networks and need the support of the community around them.

This consensus has only partially caught on, however. The Empowerment Zones and Enterprise Communities instituted by the Empowerment Act of 1993 provide tax credits and other incentives to business in distressed communities. The act contains language about community involvement as a prerequisite for planning how a local zone will use its money, but the processes are often long, cumbersome, and filled with rancor. Neighborhood leaders are often encouraged to try to adapt to regulations rather than to what good business sense would require of them.

If the government would designate cities with significant pockets of poverty, or even certain areas within those cities, for tax advantages, then citizens and developers who are willing to risk capital could drive the recovery. The current system often drives neighborhood activists to spend an extraordinary amount of time chasing federal rules and money. Targeting communities with strict boundaries within a city creates dislocations within regional economies and, to date, has not demonstrably proved to be effective.

To this end, Michael Porter has written that "a sustainable economic base can be created in inner cities only as it has been elsewhere created: through private, for-profit initiatives. A sound economic strategy must focus on the position of inner cities as part of regional economies, rather than treating inner cities as separate, independent economies; otherwise, economic activity there will not be sustainable."[4] This statement is backed up by evidence showing that minority, and primarily African-American, businesses are more successful when they move to thriving suburban economies than when they remain in targeted "enclave" economies such as those created by empowerment zones.[5]

Pouring money into urban areas without tying them to the larger metropolitan economy through joint ventures, strategic alliances, and subcontracting relationships will not change the position of those areas. And the people who live there ultimately lose out. While empowerment zones require the participation of local residents in the planning process, the participation is accomplished within the narrow confines of federal regulatory requirements and without much incentive to connect residents to larger employment and enterprise opportunities.

Economic empowerment is best thought of within the context of building social capital. Creating opportunities for residents of distressed communities is as much about helping them get connected to networks as anything—networks of employers, business partners, providers of financial capital, vocation-enhancing education, and supportive-services providers such as job training and other skills-development agencies. It is through networks that people learn the norms of the workplace and the expectations of business partners. The role of community-based organizations in this context is to help make the connections and provide whatever support is needed to help people discover a sense of purpose that guides vocational choices.

### Municipal Citizenship as Classical Empowerment

No one has written about "classical empowerment." I call it "classical" because it is not new but merely the application of some good, proven ideas. It combines the best elements of empowerment in the varying models mentioned previously. It stands on the shoulders of a long American tradition that prizes a shared sense of ownership for communities between government and private citizens, a dependence on values and virtue, and a market that is open to all.

In short, classical empowerment tries to develop the best possible relationship between neighborhood residents and government, the market, and nonprofit community organizations—the three main sectors of society.

*Shared vision, not political power-seeking.* Rather than promoting the political activist version of empowerment, we sought to create ways for public officials and private citizens to come together to solve problems that they both cared about. Political battles will always be with us, because there will always be strong differences of opinion on important matters. But any city has issues and opportunities that can be addressed more effectively through cooperation than power grabbing. There is no purely Democratic or purely Republican way to fix a crumbling sidewalk, just as there is no purely public or purely private solution to crime. These matters are dealt with best when a shared vision drives the agenda.

*Value-shaping organizations, not just any organization.* It is easy for Toquevillians to adopt a blind admiration for local and community-based organizations. There is certainly a virtue to the small scale of neighborhood and other community institutions, but smallness by itself does not renew cities or solve problems. Value-shaping organizations, such as faith-based and other organizations that encourage good works among their members and in their community, are especially important agents of empowerment. Not only are they small and close to people in need, but they hold the community as a whole to higher standards. They see a job not merely as a source of income but also as a source of dignity. They demand not only that at-risk youth stay in school but also that they have mentors. They regard the children in their day-care center not merely as sources of revenue but as unique members of society worth investing in.

*Economic opportunity, not just money.* Money by itself never solves much of anything. It is what is done with money and what money encourages that counts. Any city that cares about its citizens who occupy the margins of opportunity owes it to them to build a strong citywide economy. Too often, there is an "us-them" fight in cities between the primary beneficiaries of a strong economy and those who are marginalized. Any attempt to build a strong citywide economy looks, justifiably, like nothing other than the rich trying to get richer. That is why it is imperative that a lot of creative energy is invested in network building between those on the margins and those in the mainstream. For most people, economic well-being comes from access to education, social networks where jobs are found, capital, and good advice. The same should go for the economically disenfranchised.

In summary, classical empowerment's strength is that it is comprehensive enough to address a city's complex needs. The trouble with political empowerment as a lone strategy is that it rests on the singular goal of capturing an existing political post or strongly influencing those that have political power. This may end up doing little for neighborhoods' primary civic and economic needs, and it usually only fuels divisiveness. Purely democratic empowerment, such as the Toquevillian view, believes that citizens should be engaged in community issues no matter what, and whatever follows is the best thing—which we know is often not the case. Focusing solely on mediating institutions, with the hope that citizenship will be revived as a result, can be done wrongly. And the trouble with a purely economic view of empowerment is that it assumes that infusing money and jobs has to happen before any social capital can be built.

If empowerment is about improving civil society, it has to combine the best of these different views. Moreover, it has to carry them out simultaneously. In Indianapolis, we needed to make resources available to neighborhood associations at the same time that we were requiring them to take on more responsibility for enterprise and ingenuity. Leadership among city residents was developed at the same time that they were being asked to sit at the table with city officials to determine what was best for their neighborhoods. Their associations needed help getting organized to manage newfound responsibilities at the same time that public officials began making requests of them. All of these things needed to happen at the same time but without ever losing sight of the most important thing: successful empowerment depends on greater responsibility among city residents and greater outreach and inclusion of them by city officials at all levels of decision-making.

Classical empowerment focuses on the goals of self-government, self-sufficiency, and high levels of citizen participation in the public process. It holds that power does indeed need to transfer to citizens where it is monopolized by government, but it does this without creating sharp "us-and-them" lines between city and citizen, bureaucrat and taxpayer, governor and governed. Its proper environment is the community as a whole, not one sector or another. Classical empowerment seeks to achieve an active balance between each individual's good and the community's good, and between private and public action.

## Recovering a Robust Civil Society in Indianapolis

Confident in these assumptions, we launched the Neighborhood Empowerment Initiative in Indianapolis, which had municipal citizenship as its goal. The initiative could easily be replicated, or improved on, in large and small cities across the nation. We were on the constant lookout for ways that we could help people gain more control over their neighborhoods and be given real authority over services and programs that affected them.

Four guiding maxims shaped all Neighborhood Empowerment Initiative activity. It is one thing to be able to articulate the basic principles of classical empowerment. It is easy to say that citizens need to be at the table when important decisions are being made. It is quite another to translate these principles into action. The following four maxims set the parameters for the way we structured the initiative, and they too are portable to other communities.

*1. If we really believe that residents in possession of adequate information know what's best for their community, we have to prove it through our outreach and ability to listen to them.*

Years of top-down solutions and programs designed from within the high walls of city hall create habits that die hard. Some of these habits result from the monopolistic nature of the bureaucracy. Additionally, habits develop as professionals experience disappointment with neighborhood leadership that they thought was entirely avoidable.

The most important thing to be done to change these habits is to force public officials into situations where they have to develop personal relationships with neighborhood leaders and residents. We noticed that once this was done, city officials enjoyed their work more thoroughly. Outreach to citizens does not mean that public officials have to check their knowledge and skills at the door and simply follow the people's wishes. Residents need help knowing what their options are in each situation that involves government, how to proceed, and the best way to get the results they are looking for.

We undertook a massive physical infrastructure improvement program at the same time we began our empowerment initiative, and it included rebuilding all the playgrounds and parks. A gentleman from our parks office went to a neighborhood meeting with plans for the parks in a particular neighborhood, and the residents said, "We don't want the playground there. And we want basketball, not baseball." When he explained to me what had happened, I advised him to listen to the residents, and he went back to the residents and asked specifically what kind of park they wanted. They responded, "How should we know? We're not park designers."

Obviously, there was a role for each party to play. The residents knew the issues facing their community and could explain how the park could best meet their needs once they understood what their options were. The key was to have the park official understand their concerns about their youth, their seniors, the kinds of activities that were missing in their neighborhood, and so on, and he could then work with them to design the best park for them. The park officials, however, had a budget for the entire city and had to remind residents to stay within what was possible. Planning has to start with the amount of money available and set priorities accordingly. Open-ended planning is frustrating and unfair to both sides.

This type of interactive process ran through stages. The first voices public professionals hear may be louder, less representative, and more narrowly focused than they would like. Residents, not unreasonably, are often driven by a specific land-use issue near their property. However, a constant effort to recognize and legitimize community leaders gives them the authority and willingness to fashion appropriate compromises. This outreach also must encourage citizens to participate and lead. They have to be allowed to make real decisions, including those involving the priority and allocation of public resources. They have to learn how to create the delicate balance between consensus and leadership in their neighborhood, which is necessary to prevent inertia and produce the kinds of results that keep them engaged and wanting more. When city hall produces results in response to this leadership, it enhances the work of the leader and neighborhood and creates a reservoir of goodwill on which the leader can draw in mediating difficult challenges. As neighborhood leaders emerge, the results can be encouraging.

We invited many other neighborhoods to organize themselves and come forward with issues they wanted us to deal with. Clara Warner, president of a near-north side neighborhood association, gathered other association presidents for a citywide meeting on the increasingly bad drug problem we were experiencing. They wanted a new policing relationship, with explicit participation by both the community and police. Thus they met regularly until they had completed a "Memorandum of Understanding" in which they outlined their roles and the roles of the police, the prosecutor's office, the health department, and my office.

After helpful negotiations during which residents came to understand police resources and police better understood neighborhood frustrations, all parties signed the memorandum. It became a guiding document for the city's overall approach to eradicating crime. The subsequent drop in crime produced a victory for all partners, which in itself was the kind of victory that strengthens a city and motivates even more positive action.

Neighborhood leaders eventually participated in interviews for new officers or even a new chief. Olgen Williams, director of the very active Christamore House, a community center, and former president of the near-west side neighborhood association (featured in the case study at the end of this book), has said, "Our neighborhood controls our destiny. We got to interview the new police chief, and ensure that he was community policing-minded. When we were having repeated problems outside a local liquor store, the city helped us learn how to remonstrate against a new liquor store permit. We collected crime statistics. We testified. We closed that liquor store. We've been taught how to work together. We don't fool with politics. We just know what we need."

*2. Neighborhood participation does not automatically work by inviting citizens to the decision-making table. It requires training, resources, partnerships, and accountability that help community leaders adequately convert their knowledge and concern about the area into results.*

This maxim has to do with building the atrophied muscle tissue I mentioned earlier. In order to provide the help that neighborhoods needed to build leadership, several things were needed. First, these local organizations needed some requisite size and capacity. We undertook supporting them aggressively without co-opting their role as community leaders free to express their grievances to us. We helped them recruit funds from foundations rather than simply accept grants from us. We helped United Way fund a training academy and made sure the board was made up of neighborhood association leaders. A variety of resources were broken into small amounts that nevertheless allowed the community organizations to stimulate activity and create results. We accomplished this in various ways, from public art grant programs to $5,000 beautification grants funded from fees on developers seeking tax abatements.

The city helped solve the highest profile neighborhood problems by responding to the indigenous leadership. They told us which were the worst sidewalks and streets, identified areas where beautification would be most recognized, and pointed out the abandoned buildings most in need of demolition. Neighborhood advisory groups prioritized complaints for city crews.

Residents also needed training in effective leadership skills. I watched as one of the country's premier CDCs ran into troubles when its activities began outpacing the depth and breadth of its management. It got itself engaged in too much too fast, and the management did not have the ability to order the organization strategically. The hardest-hit neighborhoods face the most complicated problems, and they usually do so not only with scarce financial resources but also with a shallow leadership pool. This requires a lot of intentional assistance by those in a position to help.

With local funders and the United Way, we created a training academy called the Neighborhood Resource Center. This center, controlled by a board of local officials, teaches essential skills to neighborhood organizations and leaders, and it provides residents with ongoing workshops, technical assistance, and a variety of other useful opportunities.

We also brought Robert Woodson and several of his colleagues from the National Center for Neighborhood Enterprise to conduct workshops for citizens in which they could learn how to build sustainable grassroots organizations. This was valuable from two standpoints. For one thing, the actual knowledge transfer was valuable. Neighborhood leaders learned a lot that they could turn around and apply in their communities. But just as important was the inspiration that came from hearing Woodson talk about how empowerment was possible—that it was a reality within their reach, and that they owed it to themselves to throw themselves into action.

On another front, a housing intermediary, the Indianapolis Neighborhood Housing Partnership (INHP), helped leverage tens of millions of dollars into homeownership and worked closely with our CDCs. Its leaders had grown increasingly concerned about the capabilities of the fourteen CDCs in its network to keep up with the complicated demands placed on them from all sides. The increase in housing production greatly lagged the increase in public dollars invested. This presented us with a predictable clash between those in city hall demanding the kind of performance that should follow the responsible use of public dollars and those in the neighborhoods demanding more autonomy and authority. This prompted a two-pronged response from the city. We ratcheted up performance demands by making future funding dependent on the previous year's results. INHP also sponsored a million-dollar training effort to bring the uneven skill levels of the CDCs up to the level necessary to serve their neighborhoods well. Higher expectations combined with better preparation to set new standards.

In addition to training, the neighborhood groups and many CDCs simply lacked the necessary bodies to do the work. The city helped raise foundation dollars, with the lead taken by the Annie E. Casey Foundation, which provided a coordinator for each neighborhood. The critical factor in making coordinators successful was that they worked for the neighborhood and not the city. At the beginning, the neighborhoods were not ready to think strategically, and some of the plans they outlined did not seem to get at the heart of the problems they were facing. While we honored their plans, the coordinators and other consultants would work with the residents to help them understand what was realistic, what was not, and what kinds of help they could count on receiving from the city. The coordinators were a daily bridge between the formerly disparate worlds of neighborhood and city hall.

*3. Measure and demand performance.*

It is necessary for a city administration to demand performance when it funds a community effort. Too often, the importance of nurturing leaders and developing political capital dissuades city officials from blowing the whistle on failure. This process is unfair to the leaders and their communities. Clear accountability for results, not the micromanagement of inputs, will encourage tangible outcomes in a community and produce more respect for the leaders. In any city there are great variations in capacities among neighborhood organizations, CDCs, and faith-based groups. Sending a signal that performance matters will likely attract groups that already care about results and help avert future failures.

A performance culture needs to maintain a balance between two things: realistic expectations and high standards. We saw some CDCs spend twice as much as an average homebuilder constructing a house—and doing so at a slower pace and with less quality. No single standard in a case like this, such as being faster or cheaper than average, is as important as having a coherent process in place for measuring and rewarding performance. A CDC or neighborhood group may not have the human or financial resources to improve much beyond where it currently performs. If this problem is not directly confronted, then expectations need to be set accordingly.

Frequently, however, the available resources in an organization clearly demand higher performance. We saw some spectacular failures among CDCs that became increasingly ambitious while lacking the ability to fulfill their goals. They would spend a significant amount of money on staff and overhead while producing only a few houses every year. It is not at all unreasonable, we learned, to establish ambitious productivity standards while respecting the inherent limitations of community development groups. What is important is that everyone knows the standards in the beginning, that a process is set up to monitor progress, and that early warning procedures are established so that deviations from the standards can be detected and fixed as early as possible.

I committed the city to a high standard of responsiveness early on when I told the neighborhoods, "You decide what you want to do, and I'll get the bureaucracy out of the way." Bureaucrats needed to have performance goals that were congruent with the goals of the people they were trying to help, and they needed to be held responsible for what happened in specific neighborhoods. It is difficult to come up with a universal template for performance in urban revitalization efforts. What is more important than the template used is the way that the promises between the city and the neighborhoods are communicated and upheld. If building trust by keeping promises is the first priority, and if breaking trust is penalized, the best performance standards make themselves known.

*4. Government should take an appropriate supportive role. It must provide security and other core public goods, supply sufficient funding for parks, roads, and "gap" financing to help with housing and economic development.*

Public investment in core services is important for attracting private investment to an ailing community. It is also symbolically important as a statement of confidence in the area. We learned that our investments in troubled neighborhoods provided hope to homeowners and businesses that their investments would pay off in the future. They would begin to believe that their property values would go up again, and this motivation alone would begin to generate new kinds of care for personal property. Neighborhood revitalization and innovation cannot be disconnected from future economic consequences, and government has an obligation to make sure that this connection stays strong or is repaired where it is lacking. Government professionals need to be able to justify public investments in terms of the additional investment they are likely to attract, and then use this information to help neighborhood leaders make the best decisions for their community.

This usually requires activity on multiple fronts. As we began a massive infrastructure project that replaced sewers and sidewalks, we started coordinated enforcement projects that actively used residents in the effort to pressure the city and the courts to do a better job removing negative influences from their neighborhoods. Code-compliance committees in various neighborhoods brought together multiple agencies to assist residents in identifying and eliminating code violations, for instance. These important, citizen-driven groups made neighborhoods more attractive to businesses and encouraged private personal investment in property improvements.

Often government can help by providing the expertise that allows local residents to turn their concerns into results. For years in Indianapolis, community leaders complained about the awful effect of neighborhood liquor stores. One retail chain in particular did not maintain its stores. It permitted loud loitering and generated several other regulatory complaints. Yet, the residents had long been unable to turn their anxiety into a successful legal strategy against the well-financed legal team on the other side. We assigned an energetic police department civilian as a liaison and paid an attorney to help. The newly energized neighborhoods suddenly became more successful. They gathered evidence, documented their concerns, and argued their case in licensing hearings. The tide rapidly turned. Once the first store closed, others cleaned up their act, and the offending owner sold the remaining locations.

Similarly, a group of residents in another area chose to target houses that had been illegally subdivided into overly dense, often drug infested, units. Their vigilance in their neighborhood and their organization of information and observations, coupled with persistent advocacy, created a substantial change in city policy and attention to similar cases. City and private work crews became responsive to citizen priority lists of lots and abandoned houses that needed cleanup or demolition.

In another highly visible area, rundown commercial sites led to a special project. We established a Commercial Façade Design and Building Rebate Program that provided grants up to $10,000 to business owners who would complete exterior renovations on their property. In five years, we made more than $750,000 grants in order to help very visible, but decaying, corners motivate a spirit of change around them by improving their façades. The rehabilitation of an old theater in a transitional neighborhood immediately brought other investments. An older, small, African-American newspaper completely redid the front of its building and stood shining in the middle of an area that gradually followed suit by eliminating signs of decay and making a variety of improvements. In order to build an economic base in a depressed neighborhood, that neighborhood has to become a business-friendly place. In the final analysis, only an energetic citizen base that takes on projects with a clear vision of the neighborhood's potential can ultimately make the neighborhood friendly to enterprise. Government's job is to help make the supportive investments without which the citizen base cannot complete its objectives.

These guiding principles formed the platform on which all our other efforts stood. Civil society was one of our organizing principles from the beginning, but by itself, "civil society" can be a vacuous expression. Our approach to recovering a strong civil society in Indianapolis was principled and built on the premise that high standards of responsibility are both desirable and better for people. A strong municipality requires citizens, not merely just taxpayers and recipients of public services. The root of municipal, *munus*, means "duty" in Latin. Municipal citizens understand that the health of a city rests upon the degree to which they actuate their duty to the city and each other.

In the process, we have learned two very important lessons. First, our approach has helped us to see a broader, older conception of the word *public*. When citizens and government officials are working together in a way that empowers, we move beyond the overly simple distinction between "public" and "private." For municipal citizenship, "public" no longer simply means anything that is paid for with tax dollars and run by bureaucrats. It is bigger than that. It includes the common good of citizens as well. In our city, when government officials and private citizens worked together on common projects, the term "public sector" seemed a little artificial. There are obviously clear lines between what is the government's jurisdiction and what is not, but when citizens are empowered, they begin to view the community as a whole as a "public square" over which they have some control and influence.

Second, active and empowered municipal citizens are the best guarantee against social pathologies and the economic cost that surrounds them. They enforce codes of conduct in their neighborhoods that were previously absent, whether that means breaking up groups of young people gathered on high-crime corners late at night or making absentee landlords accountable by forming code-compliance committees. They ensure a collective knowledge that is greater than that of government workers. They usually provide more carefully crafted solutions to problems than when government officials solve problems on their own. And when they generate pride in what they have become and attract attention, they are magnets for an abundance of opportunities. We learned that businesses, colleges, and effective nonprofit organizations are eager to partner with successful community groups. Success breeds future success as social networks grow stronger and wider, and the wider community begins to think of the neighborhood not in terms of its costs but its value.

*Endnotes*

[1] Robert Weissberg, *The Politics of Empowerment* (Westport, Conn.: Praeger, 1999), 54.

[2] *Ibid.*

[3] *Ibid.*, 83.

[4] Michael Porter, "New Strategies for Inner-City Economic Development," *Economic Development Quarterly* 11, no. 1 (1997), 12.

[5] See, for instance, Scott Cummings, "African-American Entrepreneurship in the Suburbs: Protected Markets and Enclave Business Development," *Journal of the American Planning Association* 1, no. 1 (1999).

# SECTION TWO
# Indianapolis as a Laboratory

## Chapter Three

# Building Strong Neighborhoods I

### *Solid Infrastructure, Strong Local Economy, Safe Streets*

Adam Smith was only somewhat optimistic when he said that little else was needed to move society from violence and incivility to affluence and well-being "but peace, easy taxes, and a tolerable administration of justice, all the rest being brought about by the natural course of things."[1] As a mayor, I could have used a little more help from "the natural course of things," but Smith was basically right. Safe streets, tax rates that businesses and residents can live with rather than run away from, fairness in rewarding what is right and punishing what is wrong—if government can get these basics right, civil society will be strengthened in the end.

Big-city mayors in the 1970s and 1980s, with the best of intentions, attempted to purchase their way out of problems with increasingly bigger, more substantial government interventions. Wealth redistribution became more aggressive. Federally financed help became more dominant, sometimes through direct subsidies like welfare and sometimes through federally reimbursed bureaucratic interventions, such as child welfare programs that responded to parental violence and neglect.

Over time, it became increasingly evident that this approach was failing. In the early 1990s a new group of mayors took over who, according to social critic Myron Magnet, built a "new urban paradigm." This group, Democrats and Republicans alike, wanted to get the basics right.

They tackled problems like crime, high taxes, and poverty by reversing the ways in which government was actually perpetuating the problems rather than helping to solve them.

The group of mayors, of which I was privileged to be a part, saw that instead of limiting government's range of activity to what it does best, it had limited its effectiveness by trying to do too much or do the wrong things or both. It had gotten the job of governing backward: instead of helping to solve problems, its interventions often exacerbated problems. Good intentions were stifled by bad ideas and damaging practices. It is ironic that the time-tested basics of a limited and effective government would be called a "new paradigm."

Among the characteristics Magnet attributes to the new urban paradigm are new ways to combat crime, welfare dependency, and bloated city governments that are wasteful and destructive to the local economy.[2] From New York City to Philadelphia to Milwaukee, mayors began to recognize that conventional methods of tackling these problems were in serious need of reassessment.

In Indianapolis, we saw early on that much of what was wrong about these methods of problem solving was precisely their focus on problems. They often neglected a community's real assets—from community groups to physical infrastructure such as parks to strategic business locations—which, if made the center of empowerment strategies, could help eliminate problems.

The standard problem-oriented approach to urban ailments usually exacerbates whatever it claims to be fixing. Too many people living in poverty? Increase welfare benefits and organize campaigns to get people signed up for additional benefits. Too little revenue? Raise taxes and then criticize the businesses and the people that leave the city as the "bad guys" who make tax hikes necessary. These standard ways of doing things were far more destructive than helpful.

The neighborhood revitalization that we undertook in Indianapolis wove together many threads but, fundamentally, it recognized that the disintegration of urban neighborhoods creates a malaise—a lack of confidence, participation, and investment. This pathology causes people to leave, invites in drug dealers, decreases the value of existing property, and intimidates bankers and businesspeople. Those with some wealth are the most mobile and leave first. Well-educated young professionals also flee, and lower-income elderly people, whose houses make up a high percentage of their assets, cannot financially afford to stay or leave.

This downward spiral picks up speed as those with resources, who are able to leave a community that is perceived to be slipping, generally do in fact move. Positive momentum requires a combination of responses.

Creating a positive influence requires a blend of public and private commitments oriented around assets, not liabilities.

Six months into office, in July 1992, I sent out a letter to community leaders explaining that my administration was going to pursue an "empowerment model based on assets rather than problems." We were committed to increasing the financial, human, and social capital within our communities instead of spending money on specific programs aimed at the symptoms of specific problems. The old welfare system saw poverty as a purely economic problem that cash assistance could solve. It degraded local assets and rewarded inappropriate behavior. Crime-fighting systems depended on rapid response to dispatched calls after crimes were committed, and it devoted almost no time or resources to crime prevention and problem solving.

In short, conventional solutions to urban problems since the 1960s were usually reactive and passive. They were not strategic and forward-looking. And because they lacked vision, they were cruel. They demonstrated little concern for urban residents' well-being over time and implicitly assumed—despite the rhetoric in which they were conveyed—that "damage control" was the job of social policy.

## Citywide Reform as a Way of Life

The neighborhood reforms we undertook were part of the larger effort to create a successful city and thus the approach to urban renovation needed to be part of that effort, not distinct from it. The vision for the city and these neighborhoods was stamped on signs, hung in hallways, and placed on letterhead. It greeted every visitor to the mayor's office in city hall. It was simple, yet it stated clearly where our priorities lay:

> *A Competitive City*
> *with Safe Streets,*
> *Strong Neighborhoods,*
> *and a Thriving Economy*

Everything we did fell under these three umbrella goals: safe streets, strong neighborhoods, and a thriving economy. The organizing principle was competition. Competition, we knew, is the engine that drives excellent performance. We wanted to be a competitive city at two levels. We worked to be competitive *as a city*—that is, we wanted to be regarded as possessing unique advantages when compared to other cities and regions. We also wanted competition to drive our provision of services, whether we were providing them ourselves or coordinating their provision through private vendors.

Today, competition through privatization has grown to be commonplace, at least in theory. In 2000 I was part of a group of mayors and governors who each wrote individual chapters in a book entitled *Making Government Work: Lessons from America's Governors and Mayors*.[3] Six of the eighteen chapters include the word *privatization* or one of its cognates in their titles. Three more, including mine, use the word *competition* or one of its cognates. Half of the book, then, is explicitly dedicated to state and local efforts to introduce nontraditional service providers into the public provision of services—all with the goal of cutting government wastefulness and, at the same time, improving service quality. Compared to ten years earlier, when a few academics and public officials were only talking about these things, this book sheds light on how far we have come in a relatively short period.

I spent about one-third of my book, *The Twenty-First Century City: Resurrecting Urban America*, talking about the way we introduced competition into city government in Indianapolis as a way to improve performance and cut unnecessary costs. That book, along with the chapter in the previously mentioned book, lays out in great detail what was involved in the competition process, what we learned, and what kind of success we enjoyed as a result. I do not need to repeat the story here. But a few points are in order.

"A competitive city," in our understanding of the term, applied to more than the cost cutting associated with nuts-and-bolts services such as trash collection and street repairs. Sure, it applied to competition with our suburbs and other cities, but it also meant that our own citizens should have competitive choices in all kinds of services. For example, it applied to heightened levels of accountability in human services as well, and it meant that a broad range of formerly excluded service providers could enter the mix. Competition within a city improves services and drives down costs for residents. And of course, competition with other cities for business and market sectors creates new jobs and wealth for residents.

For example, we insisted from the beginning on performance standards for our welfare-to-work initiatives. We brought in America Works, a for-profit job-placement firm that receives payment only after it has successfully kept people employed for four months, to create a competitive workforce development climate. And our competitive approach to service provision opened up new opportunities for minority-owned businesses and nonprofits to bid on contracts. Both of these aspects—accountability and new opportunities—will be discussed in detail later.

A market-based approach to government service has its critics. But the goal of competition is not merely to apply, as I have sometimes heard it said, the "harsh reality" of the market to government. It is a means by which the shared values of responsibility and accountability are implemented in government business. It is also a means of opening up opportunity to new service providers. This effort caused even our own workers to become more responsive to neighborhood concerns, monitoring their complaints and working diligently to correct them.

Our revitalization effort combined restoring hope for improving the quality of life with increasing the stakes and responsibility of all involved. It consisted of the following components:

- *Enhancing Neighborhood Appearance*
- *Increasing Economic Opportunity*
- *Creating True Community Policing Partnerships That Enhance Safety and Foster Mutual Respect*
- *Strengthening Neighborhood Independence and Self-Governance*
- *Increasing the Impact of Faith-Based Organizations*

I will treat the first three points in the present chapter and will address the last two points in Chapter Four.

In Indianapolis we knew that if we wanted to empower residents to have a decisive voice in affairs that affected them, we needed to be doing other things that complemented this work. Residents will not be motivated to take control of their neighborhoods if their sidewalks are crumbling and their parks are unfit for their children's use. They will not see the point in improving their community if the surrounding local economy offers little hope. It was simply unreasonable to ask residents to take on a greater share of responsibility in their neighborhoods without a concerted effort on our part to make our community a place worth being involved in.

In order to get an effective empowerment initiative off the ground, then, we began several other citywide initiatives to build up crumbling infrastructure, energize the economic base, encourage a results-driven workforce-development culture, and make life difficult in general for people who break laws and threaten the well-being of others.

## Enhancing Neighborhood Appearance

### Building Better Neighborhoods

One of the most important projects to which we applied the savings that our competition of government services generated was our Building

Better Neighborhoods initiative (BBN). It was the largest capital-improvement project in Indianapolis's history. To fund that effort, we borrowed against the savings and refinanced existing city debt. That approach differed greatly from conventional wisdom. In 1991, about six months before I was elected mayor, the Indianapolis Chamber of Commerce released a report called "Getting Indianapolis Fit for Tomorrow" (GIFT). It called on the city to spend $1.1 billion over ten years to repair Indianapolis's aging streets, bridges, sidewalks, sewers, parks, and buildings. It also proposed that the city fund the improvements through a variety of tax and fee increases.

GIFT, not ordinarily the kind of present a newly elected mayor likes to receive, presented the city with a challenge it could not ignore. But while the report was right to identify the needed infrastructure improvements, it was not right to suggest that taxes had to be increased, which would have most harmed the poorest neighborhoods. By the end of 1999, when I left office, BBN had spent more than $1.3 billion on capital improvements, without any increases in city taxes.

It was important that the physical improvements increase confidence and investment across the city. To that end, we made sure that local leaders were included in the planning of projects and had ample opportunity to provide input on where to spend the money. Shortly after I was elected, I went across the city, meeting with residents and community and business leaders. They were all excited about the prospect of repairing our ailing infrastructure, because they knew better than anyone how closely it was tied to the value of their property and neighborhood in general. I remember when one resident arrived at one of our town hall meetings with a crate filled with chunks of his crumbling sidewalk—as if to make sure we understood that infrastructure repairs were not an option but a necessity.

The $1.3 billion BBN program was a citywide initiative, but we concentrated the work in the most distressed neighborhoods. Residents who live in poorer communities often resent improvements that take place in commercial districts, especially when they have not seen city investment in their neighborhoods for a long time. City officials can talk until they are blue in the face about how their city's future depends on successful commerce, but residents of distressed communities will not care.

Our distressed communities felt immeasurably distant from city hall, and we knew that residents in those communities would not be interested in our empowerment efforts if we did not invest in the repairs that their neighborhoods needed. It was therefore important that physical improvements in the targeted inner-city areas occurred quickly, visibly, and *before* any downtown construction began.

Between 1992 and 1999, we had repaved over 2,100 lane-miles of roads, repaired 1.6 million feet of curbs and sidewalks, connected 3,500 homes to sanitary sewers, improved 141 bridges, and improved or opened fourteen swimming pools and 131 playgrounds. No other capital improvement program had been so aggressive or so widespread in the city, and none had ever invested so much in our city's low-income neighborhoods.

Clearly, though, if a sidewalk or park were repaired and nothing else occurred in the neighborhood, little of long term value would be created. Thus, it was important to leverage the capital investments in a way that encouraged local leaders and residents to care about the community's future.

### Project 180

In 1994 I was on an airplane flying to Washington, D.C., and recognized the executive director of Keep Indianapolis Beautiful, a nonprofit organization committed to the aesthetic enhancement of our city. I asked him how our construction plans might generate volunteerism that would lead to cleaner and more attractive communities. During the flight, we conceptualized Project 180, a collaborative effort that would enlist the support of businesses, neighborhood groups, schools, and government.

Project 180 rallied these diverse groups together to carry out beautification projects that employed youth, involved volunteers from the neighborhoods and participating businesses, and in general focused on increasing community pride. It took a holistic approach to neighborhood improvement and concentrated on fixing up houses, community facilities, and green spaces.

The effort took off quickly. Between 1995 and 1999, eighty businesses committed more than $2 million in funding and in-kind services. I remember typical Saturday projects in near-downtown neighborhoods, which would attract business volunteers who, together with the residents, would be hauling dirt around, mixing paint, dragging trees to their planting sites, and joking with the youth who would show up to work. The entire crew would be supported by heavy trash trucks provided by the city and a variety of supplies donated by local corporations.

The band of volunteers would pick up trash from streets and alleys, while others would help to paint the homes of a few low-income elderly residents. There was a lot of conversation during the day, a lot of shared ideas about what would make a neighborhood better, and a lot of work that got done. Among the results of that first year:

- Nearly 200 houses were repaired and painted.
- More than 150 youth were given income opportunities.

- More than thirty community gardens were established on formerly vacant, litter-ridden lots.
- More than 1,700 trees were planted.
- More than 1,000 properties were improved.
- More than 200 private sector partners participated in the program either by making contributions, involving volunteers, or coordinating events.

David Forsell, a program director for Keep Indianapolis Beautiful, describes the significance of Project 180 this way: "New relationships are being formed that cross racial and socioeconomic lines. Youth are given constructive opportunities to make money. Other residents, businesses, and service organizations are being motivated by the program to paint houses and places of business and to plant trees near Project 180 planting projects. That's what the program is all about." I remember a volunteer on the southeast side of town remarking that Project 180 "changed a lot of attitudes about what can be done with the city and through the city." Alongside BBN, Project 180 was a way to help residents take pride in and feel ownership of the capital improvements taking place across the city.

### Mayor's Community Service Program

In areas of low homeownership, community leaders face enormous challenges. In areas where the base of property owners is low, the work required to clean up trash, remove graffiti, and repair deteriorating homes is often great. In order to motivate citizens to pitch in and help out, we discovered that leaders in these neighborhoods needed to show visible signs that progress was being made.

We thus began to search for ways of getting additional manpower to take on projects deemed worthy of pursuing by neighborhood leaders. Shortly after taking office, I created the Mayor's Community Service Program, which allowed jail inmates to volunteer to beautify common areas in neighborhoods and parks. The inmates were not forced to participate, and they did not volunteer in order to reduce their sentences. Mainly comprised of nonviolent offenders, the work crews were not escape or security risks.

We asked 200 community activists to list the most important projects in their areas and to let us know whether they would be willing to organize volunteers to carry out the project. We employed a full-time coordinator for the inmate program, selected supervisors from city work crews, retrained some city employees who had been laid off because of our privatization efforts, to be guards. The inmates gardened, weeded greenways, removed litter and graffiti from public spaces, painted buildings, and did landscaping. By 1999, they had donated more than 139,000 hours—or, put another way, more than $2 million worth of work.[4] Some neighborhood residents remarked that the inmates picked up trash as if it were their neighborhood.

Our initiatives to rebuild the city's ailing infrastructure and improve its appearance were aggressive and the results concrete, literally. We constantly worked to referee between the infrastructure needs that were most important in the eyes of neighborhood leaders and the priorities of the city engineers who professionally determined which crumbling but noncritical infrastructure needed repairing. When the repairs were important to the community, however, the stimulus was great. Residents experience their new sidewalks and parks firsthand. BBN was more than a "bricks and sticks" program. It was symbolic of a city that was looking forward, not backward. Any public official or community leader that claims to empower residents cannot ignore the physical realities of the environment in which people must live, work, and play every day.

## Increasing Economic Opportunity

### *Downtown Development*

Developing the downtown area of the city was one way to bolster both the urban economy as a whole and the job prospects for inner-city residents, and so we made it a priority. When we started, the opposition to major downtown improvements was palpable. Long neglected poor residents, many of whom were African-American, viewed grandiose, publicly financed downtown improvements as unfair to neighborhoods and predisposed to serve established, usually white, business interests. Yet, it seemed clear that the city had deteriorated from the center out and would need to be rebuilt from the center out.

What is more, the city center housed a disproportionately large percentage of poor residents who needed services, which are financed by property taxes. It also contained a disproportionately large amount of tax-exempt government and nonprofit property, which placed an additional burden on the existing tax base. For this reason, economic and retail growth, and the taxes it brought, was so important. The hospitality industry alone, which is heavily concentrated in the downtown area, provided nearly 50,000 jobs, many of which are held by struggling citizens whose first step on the career ladder is often in the restaurant, hotel, or retail industries.

Our inner-city residents needed to know that downtown development—and the jobs it created—would benefit them. They also needed to
see that the investment we made downtown occurred simultaneously
with BBN investments to the physical infrastructure in their neighborhoods. In order to create a sense of shared vision, it was necessary to link
inner-city residents to the career opportunities across our city. Before I
left office, and after a lot of hard work to create a new kind of downtown
culture, an issue of *Home and Away* remarked, "The city formerly tout-
ed as 'Indy-a-no-place' and 'Nap Town' has developed into an energetic
city packed with arts and culture, internationally known sporting
events, spirited nightlife, an eclectic collection of restaurants and stores,
and a diversity of people who make up the heart of this flourishing city."

Take the example of Circle Centre Mall, an upscale downtown retail
complex whose construction I halted when I was elected. The city had
invested $80 million in its development but had nothing to show for it
other than ugly craters in numerous city blocks. We brought in top-
notch design teams that helped us create a mall that does not look like
a mall. It is spread over several blocks and some of it "hides" behind
existing facades as the new construction flows nicely with the old. New
restaurants fill in the space between its street-level entrances. The new
mall attracted top stores and a theater, and additional restaurants continue to open. Its position and attractiveness have drawn people downtown like never before to shop, dine out, and entertain themselves until
late in the evening.

All of this means that people have begun spending more money during more hours of each day in and around the mall, which in turn means
that more and more jobs have been needed as well. The mall has
enjoyed between 12 and 13 million visitors a year, and the average visitor spends $64. Fifty-one percent of visitors come from outside
Indianapolis and spend more than $400 million annually. Employment
opportunities for inner-city residents have been created en masse.

More important is that the people who lived in the area began to
feel a sense of connection to downtown. They began to take pride in
what their city was becoming. I remember a conversation I had with a
maintenance worker at the convention center right before the NCAA
Final Four basketball tournament was due to begin. He lived in a nearby neighborhood, took the bus to his job, and exuded pride in what he
earned for his family and contributed to his city. He said that he was
proud to be earning a living not only doing what he enjoyed, but doing
so in a stimulating and exciting environment.

The downtown development efforts were successful. A recent evaluation of the city's partnership with Indianapolis Downtown, Inc., a
nonprofit organization we formed to make the downtown's success its

business, showed that for every dollar the city invested in downtown development, more than five additional dollars in cash and services were leveraged for further investment. However, it has also been successful because it has resulted in new jobs and a better environment for Indianapolis residents.

Along with the new jobs created by the burgeoning retail and services industries and the enhanced opportunities for recreation created by improved common areas, the downtown enjoyed a new focus on safety. Indianapolis Downtown, Inc. worked with the police department to establish a full-service police district downtown, link more than 500 security guards to the police department by radio, and implement a foot and bicycle patrol that increases police presence. Crime rates downtown dropped significantly as a result.

### Creating a Vibrant, Diverse Economic Environment

An aggressive approach to inner-city business development pays off. Beyond downtown, there exist numerous opportunities for companies located within the inner city to leverage their location as a business success. Local government has a responsibility to help these companies succeed. *Inc.* magazine began ranking the 100 fastest-growing inner-city companies in America in 1999. Not only were we pleased to see that an Indianapolis company took first place, but we were also very excited that EHOB, a medical-devices manufacturer, was one of three Indianapolis companies to make the list. With eighty employees, revenues of $7.5 million, and sales growth of 100 percent between 1993 and 1997, EHOB is an example of an inner-city company succeeding in a part of town that people had written off only ten years earlier.

We decided to revitalize the site after the CDC director walked me through the area and showed me how this desolate and abandoned place could be leveraged to benefit the surrounding community and the city itself. The director, Mark Stokes, said that only the city could get control of the property and assure investors that environmental and other risks would be dealt with. Thus the city purchased the land with funds from the BBN program and set about helping the CDC attract an employer to the inner city who saw the location as an asset. This process led us to EHOB, which purchased 7.5 acres of the property the city had purchased and environmentally remediated. EHOB leadership had determined that the inner city would be a place of additional labor and that locating there would motivate inner-city leaders to buy into a shared vision for the surrounding neighborhoods. The remaining land was either given to, or purchased by, additional enterprises looking to relocate or expand in the area. The company built its $1.5 million, 57,000-square-foot facility in 1996.

EHOB's founder, Dr. James Spahn, a graduate of the Indiana University School of Medicine and Ernst & Young 1998 Entrepreneur of the Year, had gotten to know the area as a medical student and decided it would be a fitting home for his growing enterprise. Our job at city hall was to help Dr. Spahn, and other entrepreneurs like him, relocate in a way that helped everyone win. EHOB's decision to move into the area attracted additional investment by other companies, which now consider the neighborhood a viable, strategic place to do business. More than this, the company has created employment opportunities for neighborhood residents, who have in turn generated additional interest in the business viability of the area through their enthusiasm.

We created a regulatory study commission in 1992 that began a massive effort to reduce the hassles to doing business in the city. We scrapped over 2,000 licenses and fees for small businesses and eliminated the need for 7,200 building permits per year. The cumulative direct savings for contractors through building-permit reform alone were $1.3 million by the end of 1999. Eliminated costs are costs that no longer need to be passed along to the consumer. The regulatory study commission applied the same rigor to everything from anticompetitive taxicab regulations to dog-licensing fees. The result has been a regulatory climate unrivaled by most large American cities.

Reducing the pressure to increase taxes was also necessary, so we had no choice but to reduce budget growth. If the city budget had grown at the rate it did in the ten years prior to my assuming office, it would have been approximately $584.2 million when I left office. Instead, it was $441.4 million, $18.3 million less than it was in 1991. The cumulative savings—the difference between budget trends and actual budgets since I took office—was $602.7 million. We cut overall city employee rolls by 27 percent between 1991 and 1999, with reductions for non-public safety workers exceeding 50 percent.

Three major factors created opportunities for inner-city residents. The good economy, with labor shortages in the suburbs, helped make urban labor availability an asset. The city's outsourcing efforts provided opportunities for small and minority-owned business. And the BBN construction projects gave us an opportunity to create programs that would recruit and train inner-city unskilled labor. It was important to leverage every single possibility to make a long-term difference and at least partially erase the despair faced in the long-neglected communities.

Orlando Jones, the head of the Black Family Forum, said that our competitive contracting would open up opportunity for minority businesses. He was right. To increase the participation of minority-owned and women-owned businesses in our contracting processes, we broke up large city contracts and created mentoring programs and construction colleges. We also eliminated burdensome bonding and insurance requirements. As a result, our contracts with minority-owned businesses skyrocketed from $1.2 million in 1992 to $33.4 million in 1998, and contracts with women-owned businesses likewise jumped, from $2 million to $17.6 million.

Once the doors of opportunity begin to open to nontraditional service providers, minority businesses, and an increasingly diverse set of entrepreneurs, a culture of innovation soon follows. This has benefits that go beyond anything anyone could have originally planned. For instance, in 1999 we received a mowing contract bid from Wheeler Enterprises, a nonprofit joint venture between the multibillion-dollar ServiceMaster Corporation and Wheeler Mission, a one-hundred-year-old Indianapolis homeless shelter. Their bid to mow several parks and roadsides in the city's central districts was superior to any others we received, and they won a $150,000 contract. Wheeler Enterprises employs homeless and other indigent individuals who have sought help from Wheeler Mission, which provides them with a host of personal supportive services. The partnership draws on the expertise of ServiceMaster in contract management and landscape business management. Together, they deliver quality service while helping people with multiple barriers to employment reach self-sufficiency.

Their contract with us enabled them to leverage other opportunities. They purchased a window-washing company to add to their portfolio of services, and two years after starting, they employed twenty people and were turning a profit. In the process, they have helped people learn to work, kick drug habits, begin saving money, and repair broken relationships. An enterprising environment, as it grows, attracts new kinds of innovative ventures, such as Wheeler Enterprises, which create economic value at the same time they are solving some of our most entrenched social problems.

Minority business initiatives need to be realistic, add true value, and be based not on quotas but on effort. By rigorously working on partnerships and eliminating barriers, significantly higher rates of minority participation were possible.

But race is not the same as place. And not surprisingly, many of the owners of the successful small and minority-owned businesses that competed for contracts did not come from the affected neighborhoods themselves. We needed to ensure that place-based efforts succeeded as well. So we asked the unions, who handle most of the city's work, to set up apprentice and outreach programs for local residents, and then we encouraged the vendors who won contracts to recruit 10 to 20 percent of their labor from these and other locally based job networks.

Businesses, as might be expected, were at first reluctant to participate in this strategy. But once the right leadership in unions and businesses championed the cause, we saw previously underemployed individuals acquiring new skill sets and putting themselves on a firm vocational path. This strategy, we found, represents a viable way to tie the city's investment to real opportunity for neighborhood residents who are disconnected from job networks.

### Indianapolis Independence Initiative

Clearly one of government's roles is to provide for the welfare of its poorer citizens. Urban policy has often acted on a pathological acceptance of the condition of deteriorating neighborhoods as inevitable and thus sees public subsidies as a way to mollify the effects of living in such places. Late twentieth-century liberals believed that the poor could only be helped through large programs. Conservatives, in their optimism about markets, have often argued themselves into the indefensible position that government should step entirely out of its role as a custodian of economic opportunity for people having trouble finding their way in the marketplace.

Neither of these extreme views gets it right. The first is unwise, wasteful, and usually ends up hurting the people it pretends to help over time. The second is impracticable, lacks compassion, and ignores the interest government should take in poverty as an economic development issue if nothing else. Our approach to welfare and poverty in Indianapolis was nonideological. That is, we based our activity on the broad consensus around the fact that people who work do better over time and that the city had a responsibility to help people find and keep good jobs.

We created the Indianapolis Independence Initiative as an effort to make sure that people needing work were finding jobs and that employers needing workers were finding employees. Unemployed people often lack access to employment networks, but it is also true that many employers often lack access to potential recruitment pools. In 1994, 15,000 Indianapolis families received Aid to Families with Dependent Children, the old welfare cash-assistance program. At the same time, Indianapolis employers had many jobs they needed to fill.

There was no reason why people who could work were not working. Pinned in a welfare system that pretended to care for them, mothers in particular faced serious obstacles in their effort to work their way out of poverty and take care of their families—something they would do if they could find a job and start climbing a career ladder. As a Rockefeller Foundation case study points out, our problem was that poverty "was becoming an economic development issue as well as a moral one. If regional employers could not find employees in Indianapolis, those who could move, would move."[5]

Evaluations of most government job-training efforts have revealed serious shortcomings in them. Generally, government-operated efforts have been long on good intentions and short on results. Too many of the programs pay for services and not for results. What's more, citizens in need of employment assistance deserve choices, and they need to be able to find work-based training efforts.

Competition, choice, and performance motivated us to bring America Works to Indianapolis. The Indianapolis Private Industry Council (IPIC), like most private industry councils in the nation at the time, already provided a host of employment-training services but hardly incorporated any competition into its selection of service providers. Much of its funding and energy was controlled by state bureaucrats, who insisted that programs follow a particular routine rather than achieve results.

We directed IPIC to stop offering direct training, and then we used funds over which we had control to offer America Works a partial payment when they helped someone find and keep a job for four months, followed by the balance after six months. We did this not only to introduce competition to the way that IPIC did business, but also because research by the Manpower Demonstration Research Corporation and others indicated that the best way to serve people was not through extensive training but by getting them into work and letting the employer train them. We then worked to change the culture of IPIC. Instead of its continuing to be a large service-providing organization, it was transformed into a broker of services. By managing competition for contracts, it shifted service provision to local private community-based organizations.

The Indianapolis Independence Initiative was based on three fundamental points:

1. **Foster Competition and Consumer Choice**. IPIC today provides no services. Aside from opening up service provision to a variety of bidding organizations, it encourages widespread community partnerships to address the needs that low-income residents have. Its job is to collect market data, and to contract for and evaluate services. The variety of services being provided has increased dramatically. One large social-service nonprofit, for instance, has partnered with small grassroots organizations, a large hospital network, and a uni-

versity to provide a broad array of different training
and placement services.

2. **Maximize Local Access**. In order to reach hard-to-
   serve populations and to strengthen the local networks that truly can look after people's needs, smaller
   community-based organizations need to enter the service provision game. IPIC worked with community
   centers that were part of the city's other empowerment efforts so that poor residents needing work could
   have essential services and help close to home. For
   example, the Career Corner was opened in an impov-
   erished near-east side neighborhood, run collabora-
   tively by a multi-service community organization and
   Goodwill Industries. These centers act as front doors,
   often contracting with others who have more experience, to provide the services.

3. **Engage the Private Sector**. By transforming IPIC
   into a broker of services, we necessarily opened the door
   to heightened private sector involvement. Besides
   America Works, several other for-profit job-placement
   companies began to bid for contracts, as did large and
   small nonprofit organizations. These organizations,
   through their networks in the business community,
   were able to connect employers to the welfare recipient
   population unlike ever before.

Once we brought America Works to Indianapolis, other local
providers who had formerly opposed performance-based contracting were
insisting that they could do better than America Works and wanted to
compete to prove it. We also attracted other outside firms to Indianapolis
because of our competitive approach. By 1998, IPIC had already ceased
all of its job-placement and retention services and had contracted them
out to more than 25 service providers. And the group of providers is
incredibly diverse, a mixture of big and small, local and national. Because
most of the organizations have locations in or near downtown and cannot
afford to open multiple sites, their partnerships with community-based
organizations were an important strategy. It enabled them to make their
services available close to where people live. Together, by the end of 1998,
all of these providers placed more than 2,100 people in jobs paying an
average starting hourly wage of $8.41 with benefits—reasonable by
Indianapolis standards and certainly better than welfare was paying.

A recent Brookings Institution report found that the number of families on welfare declined 40.6 percent in the eighty-nine urban counties containing the nation's largest one hundred cities between 1994 and 1999. This compares to 51.5 percent for all welfare caseloads in the country during this time period. In Indianapolis our welfare caseload decline was 54.5 percent, better than the national average and almost equivalent to Indiana's 55 percent statewide figure. The report also pointed out that urban centers have watched their share of the national welfare caseload rise considerably—from 47.5 percent to 58.1 percent between 1994 and 1999. In Indianapolis, our share of Indiana's total caseload rose almost imperceptibly, from 21.4 to 21.7 percent.[6]

Without a firm commitment to the physical and economic environment of a city, rhetoric about empowering residents will usually fall flat. More than this, residents will fall flat on their faces if there are too many holes in the sidewalks. And without access to good jobs, they may not be motivated to get up once they have fallen. Empowerment in troubled neighborhoods must stand on a sincere concern for the physical and economic circumstances of the people that live there. Our effort to rebuild ailing infrastructure and create a vibrant employment environment was as much about empowerment as about sidewalks and paychecks.

An improved physical infrastructure makes a city a more desirable place to live. It also fosters an environment in which residents begin to feel like playing a larger role. A thriving economy provides them with greater opportunities for income and choice among products and services. And a responsive workforce-development culture helps those having trouble getting connected to the economy find jobs and begin the trek up a career ladder. This all provides an indispensable backdrop to a successful empowerment effort. Empowerment requires that all these parts be moving at once. Larry Gigerich, former president of the Indianapolis Economic Development Corporation, has said, "All of these things—economic opportunity, housing repairs, business enticement, along with neighborhood capacity building and safety—are critical, and what is also critical is that all of them be done at the same time." Building a more robust civil society in Indianapolis was sort of like a juggling act. Keeping all the items moving together depends on how gracefully and accurately each one is handled.

## Creating True Community Policing Partnerships

One of the most significant areas in which communities can influence decisions that affect them is through public safety reforms. Empowerment in crime-ridden neighborhoods means giving citizens real power to proactively fight crime. This means giving them the authority to make decisions—based on their superior knowledge of the neighborhood—about how to effectively get criminals off the streets and create an environment that is pleasant to live in.

George Kelling's and James Q. Wilson's now-famous 1982 article in the *Atlantic Monthly*, "Broken Windows," argued that police would cut down serious crime if they began doing away with minor infractions. This thesis did not attract too much attention until New York City's Rudy Giuliani took it to heart. NYPD began arresting young people who routinely jumped over subway turnstiles without paying, and got off the streets the infamous "squeegee men," who jostled drivers for tips as they cleaned windshields without invitation. Signs that New York City did not care, such as the "broken windows" Kelling described, were eliminated, which made a statement to would-be criminals that bad public behavior, much less crime, was not going to be tolerated. City leaders quit pretending that crime could be driven out by a stronger economy or some other policy agenda, and they focused very hard on making crime *not* pay. Public intellectual and longtime New York City resident Norman Podhoretz captured the change well when he said,

> [I]t was itself stupid to imagine that the change in New York could all be credited to "the economy, stupid." The truth was that a majority of New Yorkers—including even liberals whispering to one another at dinner parties, if rarely in public—had finally answered my question about whether the point would ever be reached when New Yorkers would stop tolerating the intolerable.[7]

New York's success is largely a result of changes made to the police department's method of fighting crime. What is interesting about this "new" method is that urban residents have understood it to be common sense for years without needing academics to tell them about it. For decades, they endured reactive police tactics, in which police arrived only when something had gone wrong—when it was too late to stop a crime. Arresting people is not a sign of success to urban residents if the crime levels do not decrease.

For years, Indianapolis residents would complain about seedy alleys and houses that attracted illicit activity and were home to violence. They would throw up their arms as they watched youth smash out porch lights or spray paint across the side of commercial properties. They knew that if they could stop this kind of activity, they could make their neighborhood an unwelcome place for the worst crimes such as murder, rape, robbery and other kinds of assaults. But the police department worked like most city police departments: rapid response to crime, make arrests, get back to the office to fill out the papers. Police that seem not to care are another kind of "broken window" that sends a signal to criminals that crime is OK if you can run faster than the police can arrive on the scene. Nothing diminishes urban residents' confidence faster than this.

Community policing, born out of Kelling's work and further explained in his *Fixing Broken Windows: Restoring Order and Reducing Crime in Our Communities,*[8] is based on the premise that residents should not be stuck in this helpless state. They should not be in the situation of knowing what to do but unable to do it. The police should be meeting with them, listening to them, even taking cues from them. They should have their desire to prevent crime implemented into policy and action.

Our first experience with community policing came when we began in 1992 to plan for a Department of Justice Weed and Seed grant. The program's name is based on the idea that crime needs to be weeded out of a neighborhood and replaced with the seeds of positive community resources. Haughville, a near-west side neighborhood, which was riddled with bullets and infested with crack dealers, was selected as a Weed and Seed site. The planning process was perhaps as significant as anything that happened after the grant was received, because residents played a major role in outlining the terms of the grant.

Concurrent with a number of attempts to devolve authority to the neighborhood, which the residents had embraced, the Weed and Seed planning process was an example of devolution at its best. Neighborhood committees rolled up their sleeves and helped direct our police to a full-blown strategy that focused on crime prevention and positive programming. Trust that was nonexistent between the residents and the police was restored through long meetings and lots of dialogue. Before long, they knew each other by their first names, were participating in community events together. One year after residents were given the authority to design public safety policy, the number of homicides dropped within the Weed and Seed program boundaries from thirteen to one. And the numbers have continued to stay low.

We also implemented community policing in a near-north side public housing complex that is home to 650 people, Parkview Place Apartments. Residents had become fed up with the drug trafficking in the neighborhood, and police were tired of responding to a stream of constant calls about yet another shooting in the complex. Mothers were making their children sleep on the floor, where they stood a better chance of not being hit by stray bullets. A city police officer referred to the neighborhood as "a drive-through McDonald's for dope."

The apartment management, residents, and police officers came together and devised a collaborative plan to tackle the problem. The management blocked off entrances and installed speed bumps and a fence, which made the "McDonald's-like" drive-through effect disappear. Residents organized a tenants' council and a CrimeWatch group. In conjunction with local churches, the residents held after-school and summer programs for children, and they conducted neighborhood Bible studies. Working with the police, the management, residents, and churches created a list of unwanted visitors and implemented a "three strikes and you're out" policy for tenants who harbored them—which resulted in twelve evictions. The police increased their patrols in the area, got rid of abandoned vehicles, and helped the residents eliminate anything that seemed to tempt crime. Violent crime plummeted in the neighborhood, and the IPD North District was one of the national winners of the prestigious Webber Seavey award in 1995, presented by Motorola and the International Association of Chiefs of Police in honor of innovation and quality in law enforcement.

These practices have continued in our city in various shapes and styles. Some neighborhoods have their officers ride around on bicycles. Others have them back up pastors, who do the patrolling during high-crime times (which I describe later). The diversity is a reflection of who is in charge: the citizens. Citizens knew in advance what those of us formerly in charge came to understand later: public order needs to be aggressively pursued in a way that encourages good behavior and discourages bad. It would be nice if economics could solve crime problems, but it cannot. Crime is reduced when the citizens and police agree that they will not tolerate it, when they commit themselves to the belief that "things don't have to be this way," and when they work together to restore order.

*Endnotes*

[1] Adam Smith, *Essays on Philosophical Subjects*, 1795.

[2] "Introduction" to *The Millennial City: A New Urban Paradigm for 21st Century America*, ed. Myron Magnet (Chicago: Ivan R. Dee, 2000), 4-7.

[3] Eds. Paul Andrisani, Simon Hakim, and Eva Leads, *Making Government Work: Lessons from America's Governors and Mayors* (Lanham, MD: Rowman & Littlefield, 2000).

[4] The Independent Sector assigned an hourly value of $14.83 to volunteer time in 1999, calculated from the hourly wage assigned to nonagricultural workers by the Economic Report of the President, plus 12 percent for benefits ("Giving and Volunteering in the United States," Independent Sector, 1999).

[5] William B. Eimicke, Steven Cohen, and Sam Sharp, "The Indianapolis Independence Initiative," (New York: Rockefeller Foundation, Spring 1999), 10.

[6] Katherine Allen and Maria Kirby, "Unfinished Business: Why Cities Matter to Welfare Reform" (Washington, D.C.: Brookings Institution, 2000), 1, 12.

[7] Norman Podhoretz, "My New York," *National Review*, vol. 51, issue 11 (June 14, 1999): 35 ff.

[8] George Kelling and Catherine Coles, *Fixing Broken Windows: Restoring Order and Reducing Crime in Our Communities* (Free Press, 1996; Touchstone, 1998).

# Chapter Four

# Building Strong Neighborhoods II

*Enlivening Self-Governance, Increasing Social Capital, and Partnering with Faith-Based Organizations*

## Strengthening Neighborhood Independence and Self-Governance

Of course, if a city has the will to empower its most disadvantaged citizens, it must make a more intensive, concentrated effort than infrastructure and economic initiatives can achieve. Our Neighborhood Empowerment Initiative attempted to embody what I have called "classical empowerment." Classical empowerment places a greater responsibility for self-government on the shoulders of citizens, and at the same time, it requires a greater burden of obligation on government to reach out to citizens and include them in the public process.

In order to realize these two forms of responsibility, we pursued two goals, also outlined in the last chapter: to give the neighborhoods a structure with which to govern themselves more democratically and to devolve to them real decision-making authority over services that affected them. By focusing on these goals, a city administration is forced to reinvent the way it works with neighborhoods. Most cities are not in the habit of building democratic capacity and decision-making power in neighborhoods. It is much easier to stay in city hall, make policy, and only go to the neighborhoods for a press conference when a large project is being announced.

### Enlarging the Public Square

The word *public* has come to mean the realm of activity funded and managed by the government. Historically, however, it has meant more than that. The word *republic,* for instance, means "the public thing," the larger community formed by government, business, religious organizations, and other social and cultural institutions but ultimately managed by the citizens—not the government itself. Government is a custodian of "the public thing" in which all of these actors compete, cooperate, and work for both their individual good and the good of all. Government ensures liberty and equality, and it is the community vehicle through which the voice of the citizens is, or should be, fairly represented in policy.

When I took office, one of our first priorities was to break down the walls separating city hall from the residents. Before we could build neighborhood capacity for self-governance, we knew that we had to get to know the neighborhood residents, introduce our vision to them, and receive their input on it. Right away, in 1992, we started neighborhood forums. These were monthly meetings in neighborhoods across the city in which I and some other city officials would meet with community leaders and residents, present our ideas to them about giving them a greater stake in decisions that affected them, and listen to what they had to say. We did this throughout my first year as mayor, and deputy mayors continued this practice for several years following.

I had long been impressed with the community participation engineered by Dallas civic leaders, which turned the city around after the assassination of President Kennedy and became the subject of a Harvard case study. So, we launched Vision Indianapolis Tomorrow, a citywide effort facilitated by the National Civic League, which brought together leaders from across the community to construct a vision for the future of the city and build the steps to realize the vision. Hundreds upon hundreds of Indianapolis residents participated.

Much to my surprise, however, the process exposed concern that the influence of community groups that previously commanded the attention of the mayor and city hall would be diluted. It was almost as if there were only a gallon of influence available to community organizations, which would be split among contenders by the mayor, who in turn allocated amounts based on political considerations. This was very similar to the previous model of how to run a city: there is only so much wealth and it needs to be redistributed by political formulae. To us, however, civic participation was an expandable asset, a foundation upon which wealth could be created.

Neighborhood participation in neglected neighborhoods increased dramatically, but the resentment, which was sometimes based on real grievances or race or region, never fully went away. We were pleased to find, though, evaluators assessing our Neighborhood Empowerment Initiative five years later discovered that residents still talked about the neighborhood forums as significant. It had been meaningful to them that city officials sat with them in their own neighborhoods and were responsive to the concerns they expressed there. Without this period of dedicated outreach, I am not sure that our subsequent empowerment efforts would have taken root. Municipal citizenship requires that people have a stronger sense of controlling their destiny, access to needed and valuable information, and a capacity to exercise their will together and actually make a difference.

An important expression of participation is found in partnerships. Through its invitations, public recognition, and grants, city hall bestows authority and credibility on those it chooses to deal with. This authority grows if results are achieved when community-based actors petition and collaborate with city hall. Thus translating the listening to action becomes critically reinforcing. A lack of responsiveness creates the conditions by which a community begins to support leaders whose attraction is found in their open hostility to city efforts. In order to realize municipal citizenship, relationships need to be built that allow residents to modify city plans and effect real change.

### *Municipal Federalism*

Mayors across the country thought about the precepts of federalism with mixed emotions as Washington devolved more authority to states, first with welfare reform and then in a number of additional policies. These emotions were mixed because, on the one hand, top-down, centrally run programs never work well, and the state house is closer to mayors than the national capitol. Yet, on the other hand, a state bureaucrat is still a bureaucrat, even in the most positive sense of the word. My experience with some of the country's most dedicated local bureaucrats tells me that they operate at a level of geographic generality that is still too high.

Therefore, the organizing principle of our initial efforts was something we called municipal federalism. A neighborhood needs a structure to organize itself. It needs an active interface with its public officials. It needs equipped leaders. A democratic republic presupposes these ele-

ments in order to work well, and sadly, our poorest communities have
seen them vanish or be destroyed. Well-intentioned, but failed, federal
programs to relieve poverty have preyed on the lack of democratic
capacity in urban neighborhoods. Stripped of organizational and leadership infrastructure by outside authorities and out-migration, these
neighborhoods became laboratories for welfare programs and housing
failures that only made matters worse. Residents had little authority to
demand different kinds of help, because governmental authorities did
not give them authority.

The topic of federalism has enjoyed a renewed enthusiasm in the
past thirty years. President Nixon's New Federalism pushed to give
states greater flexibility in spending Washington's money, and both
presidents Reagan and Clinton issued executive orders to define the
role between the states and the federal government. Welfare reform has
been hailed as a great experiment in federalism because it gives states
greater flexibility in designing their own work-oriented welfare programs. Legislators have proposed bills to strengthen American federalism. Think tanks have announced federalism projects. Academics write
on the topic. As more and more people try to figure out how to devolve
both money and authority over programs from Washington to states
and localities, federalism has become a popular issue.

Little, though, has been done to try to experiment with federalism
at the municipal level. Historically speaking, federalism has meant
more than balancing the power between the states and the central government in Washington. In early American practice, it also meant that
vibrant local associations should play a role in the public process so
that everyday people could influence decisions about their communities. Americans formed associations to take care of a host of problems
and challenges, some in cooperation with the local government and
some apart from government simply because government was not
needed.

In my first mayoral term, after spending a year traveling throughout
all of Indianapolis's neighborhoods meeting with residents, we launched a
Municipal Federalism initiative. Our bold vision was to give neighborhood
groups much more influence over a wide range of services, from social programs to trash collection. The initiative never materialized as the robust
and comprehensive plan we had envisioned: a group of city-county councillors claimed that they were elected to represent these neighborhoods by
a democratic process that gave them the superior position in configuring
services in these areas. The argument on behalf of an elected official who
occupies the ward healer position sounded better in theory than it looked
in practice. It assumed that an election in a relatively large district is tan-
tamount to a preference about which roads get fixed.

The most aggressive residents in the Municipal Federalism effort were those on the near-west side, the West Side Cooperative Organization (WESCO) area. They wanted control over their neighborhood—full control. Because the neighborhood was in such bad shape, we had targeted it for special help early on. With help from the Annie E. Casey Foundation in the form of a planning grant, we worked with residents in the neighborhood to plan how we would tackle some of their toughest crime and social issues by giving them the power to make changes. But it was not just the early start and the additional funding that made the neighborhood unique. It had forward-looking leaders and a will to change its very difficult condition.

The leaders broke themselves down into subcommittees focused on social, safety, housing, and economic issues. They even had a "Neighborhood Governance Subcommittee" that took our idea of federalism a step further. They created block clubs with captains to serve as the representatives of their blocks to the subcommittee, which would then represent them to an umbrella organization created to manage neighborhood affairs.

Municipal Federalism was not implemented uniformly across the city, but the effort to build self-governing neighborhoods encouraged many citizens who wanted to have a greater say in how policies were put into practice in their communities. They wanted to shape the policies that touched their greatest concerns, and in troubled neighborhoods, these are often policies having to do with issues such as safety, property condition, and youth opportunities. Along with responsibility, the groups needed capacity and money to be successful.

In order to create a vibrant public square, city hall needed to continually lift up and celebrate successes. This type of recognition allowed the local leadership to showcase their accomplishments for their constituents and outside funders. On the public funding side, we created a special funding source called the Community Enhancement Fund (CEF) to serve as the basis of a refereed competition for financial awards for community-serving organizations. Having a committee comprised of a broad cross section of neighborhood and faith leaders, business executives and city officials select the winners served to transfer best-practice standards for community-based activity across the city. While we used Community Development Block Grant (CDBG) funds from the U.S. Department of Housing and Urban Development (HUD) to encourage grassroots activity, CEF funds put more resources with greater flexibility into grassroots organizations for community-building activities. We created CEF out of the fees we charged businesses applying for tax abatements.

These grants, unlike the majority of the CDBG disbursements, were small—between $500 and $5,000. Community-based organizations were given total flexibility with the funds, and they became so popular that competition for them grew fierce. Collaborations formed among community groups to try to generate more interesting proposal ideas as time moved along.

Between 1993 and 1999, we awarded more than 400 Community Enhancement Fund grants for nearly $1 million. An east-side mentoring initiative arranged for twenty high school students to serve as mentors and tutors for nearly one hundred elementary-school students. Groups turned vacant lots into parks, ugly areas into neighborhood gardens, graffiti into murals, and much more. We constantly looked for ways to devolve authority and responsibility. However, a constant tension remained between our desire to seek out enthusiastic local partners and our candid recognition of how little capacity some of them possessed.

This capacity issue would raise its head continuously. We increased the money sent to community organizations by tens of millions of dollars, and the breadth and scope of our aspirations for them similarly increased. Yet failures were not infrequent and near failures constantly occurred. Overall, though, an early concentration on capacity building did in fact dramatically increase the quality of the community infrastructure. Thus, we decided to make neighborhood capacity a central part of our entire effort. This became the common thread uniting the multiple dimensions of our Neighborhood Empowerment Initiative.

### Empowerment and Citizenship: The Neighborhood Empowerment Initiative (NEI)

Our comprehensive outreach to the community resulted in some concrete ideas for empowering residents to take control of their neighborhoods. In order to have residents capable of making significant decisions over time, they needed to have the right kind of organizational mechanisms in place. We decided to work with neighborhoods that were struggling with all the indicators of urban decay—low incomes, joblessness, family breakdown, teen pregnancy, infant mortality, high crime.

We also looked for some level of organizational capacity within the neighborhoods, whether it was in the churches, community centers, or neighborhood associations. The effort required the city and the resident leaders to create a series of organizational structures and project teams that led to, and required, partnerships in resolving problems in specific inner-city areas. Sometimes these groups were organized in ad hoc fashion around a problem, but they always built on the local leadership structures we were nurturing. There were initially seven target neighborhoods and we later added an eighth. Three of these neighborhoods are examined in detail in the case study appended to this book.

*A Sense of Place*

I mentioned earlier that the doubling of neighborhood associations while I was in office has attracted some attention. The increase in the associations signaled to us that our message was getting across. Residents had been told that they should feel free to picket city hall if they saw a need going unmet or a problem that had not been redressed. Successfully redressing a grievance may have only led to fixing a pothole or neighborhood park, but I envisioned this iterative practice of communication between neighborhoods and city hall as a way to build up the confidence of the community in itself and its leadership. Thus, we wanted the solutions to be organized and not totally fragmented. In the true sense of subsidiarity—an old concept in which authority is located at the lowest level—sometimes a block organization would have the best idea for a community initiative, and sometimes a larger community group would weave together the solution to a common problem. Therefore, we asked residents and subsidiary neighborhood groups to operate in a coordinated way.

This same principle grounded our strategy to neighborhood empowerment. We made the formation of umbrella neighborhood organizations within the targeted neighborhoods a requirement of being able to participate in NEI. The umbrella could be an existing organization that was positioned to represent the interests of the neighborhood as a whole, or it could be created.

We allocated $50,000 annually from a pool of CDBG funds to each of the umbrella organizations for them to use on projects of their choice. Other than the federal regulations that came with the funds, we stipulated only that the groups use two-thirds of their funds in collaboration with other organizations in the neighborhood. This fostered greater neighborhood activity and is a partial explanation for the increase in neighborhood groups across the city during this time.

If neighborhoods wanted to receive funding or have proposals seriously considered, they needed to operate through their umbrella organization. This did two things. First, it gave us a point of contact and a way to track any funding or activity that we directed to the neighborhood. Second, and more important (or at least more interesting), umbrella organizations forced neighborhood residents to work together, develop common aims, negotiate among themselves what kinds of programs they wanted to implement, and so on. We knew this would create some conflict within certain neighborhoods, and it did. Residents fought over the goals they wanted to achieve. Feelings got hurt. In other words, democracy was alive and well within the neighborhoods in a short time.

Some organizations chose not to become members of the umbrella organization, which allowed them to maintain their independence but also disqualified them from receiving any funds earmarked for NEI initiatives and sent through the umbrella organizations. The number of member organizations within the umbrella varied from one neighborhood to another. A near-east side neighborhood had fifteen. Another neighborhood had three. We were not interested in having hundreds of new associations for its own sake but only in so far as they enabled more and better citizen control over their neighborhoods.

The umbrella organization strategy was fundamentally important because it created within neighborhoods the kind of activity that so impressed Tocqueville when he visited America in the early nineteenth century. Partly as a response to Robert Putnam's thesis that social capital has declined in America as participation in voluntary associations has waned, some academics have argued that Americans are just as engaged as ever, albeit in larger, national membership organizations. These organizations have rivaled political parties, one academic writes, in providing "leverage in civic and legislative affairs to a large number of Americans."[1] Another writes, "Whatever the virtues of face-to-face democracy, America cannot rely entirely on institutions built around self-governance . . . The representation that is carried out by national citizen groups is more than a complement to people's civic engagement in their own communities. People who join a national citizen group are making a declaration about their political identity."[2]

And they are right—to an extent. National membership organizations provide valuable power to interests that otherwise would not make it into the parties that control the political process. And it is true that local organizations cannot influence the national political process as national membership organizations can. But what is sometimes understated by the mainstream academy, media, and government is the powerful role to be played by a strengthened local civic sector in cultivating municipal citizenship.

Fighting crime, fixing streets, preventing teen pregnancy, finding jobs—these issues themselves often drive the activity of local associations and prompt citizen engagement. Undeniably, for those of us who have worked in troubled urban areas, the decline of vibrant local associations is a stark reality. Umbrella organizations were our way of reviving a sense of community ownership and installing within neighborhoods the means for making self-governance a reality.

What strikes me about the interviews presented in the case study later in this book is the degree to which residents cite the formation of umbrella groups as a key moment in NEI. Many of the leaders in these groups were around in past failed attempts by federal programs to organize local communities. What was different about our approach (other than not having much federal money for it) was the organic quality and independence these groups had in designing what kinds of things they were going to undertake.

### Neighborhood Coordinators and Township Administrators

Neighborhood leaders spent way too much of their limited time shopping for solutions inside bureaucracies for problems affecting schools, police, zoning, public health, and more. "Bureaus," by definition, had been created for the convenience of government: highly specialized professionals could handle highly differentiated problems across a wide geographic area. The neighborhood leaders, by definition, were just the opposite: they specialized in geography and handled every public problem within defined boundaries. We needed to close the gap from both sides by setting up a better, more efficient way for the local areas to resolve their issues.

To help the organizations we set out to raise funds so that each area could employ a neighborhood coordinator. Aside from playing a critical role organizing the activities that the umbrella organization would undertake, the coordinator maintained close ties to city hall. Navigating various agencies and organizations is always difficult for volunteers. Their time and tempers run out quickly. Without the coordinator t o handle much of this work for them, many projects would not have materialized.

Public employees simply did not look on an area of the city as "theirs." We needed to have an approach based on having a person or persons responsible for an area. We formed project teams around geographic problems, which created a greater sense of ownership, and provided teams with whom neighborhood leaders could interact. For example, in conjunction with outside stakeholders, one team took a significant road artery in an area and designed economic development, park, maintenance, traffic, and commercial-façade improvements. Under the old way of doing things, this would have been done in a department-specific way rather than by a geographically based team.

We also created the position of Township Administrator and assigned one to each of ten geographic regions of the city. The administrators were responsible for finding a city hall solution to neighborhood problems. They were personalized "one-stop shops" for neighborhood residents. A leader or group, we thought, should not have to spend weeks chasing down answers to questions; rather they would call this administrator, whose job was to get the answer. They were the area's advocates inside city hall. The administrator was regularly involved in local meetings with residents, other community officials, and neighborhood association leaders.

In their first six years, the ten administrators handled 10,500 requests from neighborhood leaders for services of some sort, both big and small. The point-of-contact provided by the administrators and coordinators ensured residents that organizing around shared interests would pay off in the form of responsive action from city hall. More important, these administrators encouraged the community organizers, helped them identify solutions, and became an invaluable statement to the neighborhood about the kind of change occurring in city hall.

*Leadership Training*

Leading neighborhood revitalization is very difficult stuff. It requires urban residents to identify the right fights to pick, the right programs to address the community's needs, and the right partners to get the job done. It requires the ability to work with others, attract potential outside funders, get proposals written, comply with regulations attached to funding that comes in the door, and be an expert in many different areas from housing to welfare to transportation to child care. All of this requires leadership.

To support the needs of leadership development, as I mentioned earlier, we invited Robert Woodson and his colleagues from the National Center for Neighborhood Enterprise to lead focused training sessions, and we created the Indianapolis Neighborhood Resource Center (INRC) as a hub for ongoing training. What Woodson and his team set in motion, INRC institutionalized.

Woodson showed our residents that empowerment is a reality, not just a dream, and that a variety of skills and strategies can be learned to help residents transform their neighborhoods. INRC is a nonprofit organization that teaches neighborhood leaders about starting neighborhood organizations, managing finances, managing legal issues, recruiting volunteers, dealing with zoning requirements, and designing strategic plans. During INRC's first four years, the city invested more than $250,000 in it, which helped to leverage an additional $1 million in funds from foundations and other sources. The center worked as an academy for local leadership, with a board consisting of representatives from various organizations across the city.

Through NEI, citizens gained the opportunity to directly manage their own affairs and have an impact on decisions at city hall, but they also acquired the responsibility to develop their organizations. Because we demanded accountability from them, they found themselves needing to learn about organizational management. Anyone taking empowerment seriously also needs to take seriously the importance of supportive services that prepare ordinary residents to do extraordinary things.

### Nuisance Abatement

Creating optimism from hopelessness required identifying the most irritating and obvious community problems requiring an organized response, and then making government more effective in providing a solution. Citizens trying to keep up their area get worn down by nearby obnoxious uses of property: crack houses, vacant buildings, former stately homes subdivided into tenements, illegal dumping, and more. Getting rid of public nuisances is an important aspect of municipal citizenship in inner cities. Beyond being involved in community policing, residents need to be empowered to drive the process by which they take their neighborhoods back block by block from absentee landlords, derelict homeowners, and others whose lack of care has a negative effect on the neighborhoods. Not only do residents despise crime. They despise flat or declining property values due to unkempt properties and liquor stores that breed indecent behavior, noise, and loitering.

Code-compliance committees were one of the most popular institutions of NEI. Residents in struggling communities had long been critical of the government's response to their localized nuisance problems. And well-intentioned government officials spoke a rhetoric of powerlessness, explaining that it was another unit's problem: the courts blamed the public health officials who blamed the zoning enforcement division that blamed the poorly written laws, and so on. A coordinated approach toward mitigating these problems seemed the best way both to create hope in the areas affected and to strengthen the capacity for citizen action among residents in affected areas. Residents responded by forming committees, managed by the umbrella organization in their neighborhood, and they began to make out their lists of properties where violations posed a threat to the neighborhood's well-being. Public officials from the relevant agencies met with the teams in the neighborhood, set priorities, initiate action, and created an online tracking system that would allow the community citizens to appear in court and complain when inaction set in.

This is a good example of government playing the part of coordinator and public servant, and citizens making the key decisions that affect their neighborhood. Residents know which slumlord or violator to take on. They simply need their local government to support them in abating the problem. Once this happens, a positive ripple effect results. Residents, long neglected, achieve victory against what formerly seemed like an intractable problem, and their confidence as municipal citizens grows stronger.

Nothing sparked a sense of community victory more than a "win" against the worst of local liquor stores. As citizens realized they could take effective action on this front, new laws were passed, and teams were formed consisting of citizens, police, city lawyers, and zoning representatives. Priorities were established based on the nature of violations, land-use issues, and the effects of the violations. The politics of this activity was unpredictable. Democrat city councillors who were long critical of the stores and their effect on inner-city communities and minorities teamed with us, while others who more frequently allied with us in other battles sided with the store owners.

We passed legislation requiring liquor stores, whenever there was a liquor board hearing on new licenses or license transfers, to give fifteen days' written notice to the neighborhood associations within a mile, churches and schools within a 1,000-foot radius, and adjacent property owners. Any past legal violations by applicants had to be made known. After a decade of what seemed to be an invulnerability of the worst of the stores (some actually ran their business in a way that had no secondary land-use effect), relentless enforcement made headway in a legal system heavily stacked against the community. A dozen awful stores were closed or sold, and the areas were repaired.

These victories provided dramatic moments of success, and the practice of citizens organizing around local problems produced results in other areas. On Washington Street's near-east corridor, criminals scattered when a neighborhood business association combined the information from local citizens with the off-duty officers it hired to patrol the area and closed down some of the most popular drug-trafficking alleys. And in Mapleton-Fall Creek, an area that suffered from multiple problems, citizen-led activity resulted in 100 new apartments, 300 home repairs, and a significant reduction in murders, which were occurring once a week a decade earlier. This kind of effective action happens when organizations are given authority to direct talent, energy, and resources to the outcomes that they, not bureaucrats or alleged "experts," have identified as important. This approach can be summed up in the words of Al Polin, neighborhood coordinator for Mapleton-Fall Creek: "What works? Take organizations, find their strengths, figure out who is doing what well, support them to continue to grow. Look to the private sector as much as possible. Use the mayor's office as a bully pulpit to go out and find new resources."[3]

*Social Services*

A much more important, albeit less visible, factor in urban communities is in the area of social services. Twenty years after the success of their *To Empower People*, Berger and Neuhaus wrote that their term "mediating structures" had become so popular that it was subject to misinterpretation. Their definition, they said, had never changed: "those institutions that stand between the private world of individuals and the large, impersonal structures of modern society."[4] Along with families, congregations, and voluntary associations, Berger and Neuhaus named neighborhoods as a fourth mediating structure that provides an alternative to large-scale monopolization of social-service delivery.

The definition of mediating structure is important. A number of people have assumed that any nonprofit doing social good is a mediating structure. But not all nonprofits are neighborhood-based, and many of them deal with the same issues as impersonal government agencies. In fact, many large national not-for-profits already use significant government resources.

The twenty largest members of the National Assembly, a national nonprofit association, receive a combined $5 billion annually from government revenues, a third of their combined total revenues. Four of them receive over 50 percent of their revenues from government coffers.[5] Many of them do a great amount of good, and some have effective local programs. But these large-scale program offerings need to be decentralized at the neighborhood level, and even then, it is difficult for them to serve the truly "mediating" function of a community-based group. Federal programs exist for almost any problem a person might have, and diverse administrators run most of them according to differing rules. Many of these problems indeed might require highly professionalized service.

Our goal, then, was to decentralize outreach and supportive services, allowing a neighborhood group or faith-based organization that was better acquainted with a particular family's situation to participate in helping them. When dealing with the deepest human emotional and spiritual needs, programs cannot be run mechanically. And it is important to remember that problems such as high teen birthrates, infant mortality, poor educational performance, drug use, and crime cannot be disconnected from emotional and spiritual needs. That teen birthrates are nearly five times higher among teenage girls who have not had active fathers in their lives is a reflection that they are seeking the wrong kind of fulfillment from the opposite sex. That drug usage and the crime that accompanies it are highest in areas where economic opportunity is lowest is a reflection of a hopelessness that is rampant. Neighborhood leaders who compassionately meet these deepest needs have to be the ones to decide how social services are implemented in their community.

In some neighborhoods, community-based organizations partnered with larger nonprofits to run government-funded jobs programs. This, in turn, helped the larger organizations tailor their services to the neighborhood level. Goodwill is a good example. One near-east side neighborhood program has been running a significant job placement program with Goodwill, and a near-west side community center colocated its services with Goodwill to provide a seamless entrance into the workforce for residents participating in the center's other programs.

The Mapleton-Fall Creek Neighborhood Association, on the near north side, partnered with Goodwill's JobLink program to provide individuals with career opportunities at Clarian Health Partners, one of America's largest hospital networks. The neighborhood association was so successful, one Goodwill manager once remarked, that it became known among residents across the city as the way to get into Clarian. They know that hundreds of vocational opportunities await them by simply setting foot inside the neighborhood center, due to Clarian's commitment to help even the lowest entry-level worker dream big and climb to high-skilled, high-paying jobs.

We found that the most effective delivery of social services occurred when a local neighborhood association dealt head-on with an issue and designed its own solution. For instance, in Haughville, on the near-west side, infant mortality rates plummeted when the neighborhood began an aggressive educational program for expectant and young mothers. Neighborhood leaders decided to do what public campaigns aimed at reducing infant deaths could not do, namely engage in grassroots word-of-mouth outreach and education for expectant mothers in their community.

In another instance, we had argued for years with state welfare officials on behalf of neighborhood residents that the child protective service they administered statewide to help abused and neglected children was unresponsive and broken. It applied rules mechanically, often failing to investigate serious cases and overly intruding in families' lives in less serious cases. Residents insisted on being involved in child-protection activity in their own neighborhoods. While the state agency refused to delegate cases where child abuse had been substantiated, they did agree to jointly staff and fund a neighborhood center that would be charged with reviewing the cases and working with families in the dozens of cases that were reported but generally ignored by the bureaucrats.

Community outreach can weave together support services in a more carefully tailored way than state agencies can. This does not mean, obviously, that state agencies have no role to play. It does mean, though, that the way a service is structured and delivered on the ground matters a great deal. Grassroots private and not-for-profit participation in social-services partnerships can help increase the level of service effectiveness as well as give residents a greater stake in what happens in their communities.

## Increasing the Impact of Faith-Based Organizations

Ultimately, as much as one hopes that the market will create opportunity and neighborhoods will be energized by civic engagement, a city is only as strong as the values that animate the habits, opinions, and shared practices of its residents. One of the strongest forces holding the values of individual neighborhoods together are faith-based organizations—churches, synagogues, mosques, and other religious community-based organizations.

Often a lone anchor in their blighted neighborhoods, they measure their work not in terms of the numbers of people they serve or their cost-effectiveness, but in terms of lives transformed. From a faith stance, they help people kick destructive habits and encourage strong families. These outcomes affect the civic order, and for this reason, government has a vested interest in them, too.

But government has traditionally had little to do with religious groups, which has created an odd situation. Talented and energetic faith leaders busily improve their communities, usually without sufficient resources, and they stay away from government because the hassle of regulations usually defeats their purpose. Government, which would like to have the social outcomes that faith-based organizations produce, can navigate regulations and can provide access to resources. However, public officials usually go about trying to improve neighborhoods without coordinating their efforts with religious groups. This entire scenario, which is considered "normal" in most places, made no sense to us in Indianapolis.

We wanted to work with religious organizations to help them do their work more effectively and with greater reach. This was not, of course, a new idea. It just seemed that no one was really trying it out. In 1902, for instance, Teddy Roosevelt had said:

> The forces for evil, as our great cities grow, become more concentrated, more menacing to the community, and if the community is to go forward and not back, they must be met and overcome by forces for good that have grown in corresponding degree. More and more in the future, our churches must realize that we have a right to expect that they shall take the lead in shaping those forces for good. . . . [W]e have a right to look to the churches for

setting the highest possible standard of conduct and of
service, public and private, for the whole land.[6]

We launched the Front Porch Alliance (FPA) in Indianapolis in 1997
as a way to enhance the role of grassroots, value-shaping organizations.
Consistent with our overall approach to empowerment, we were con-
vinced that government was best positioned to take on tough social problems as a *coordinator* of services, *not a deliverer* of them. Faith-based
organizations could dream up, organize, and implement programs much
more effectively than we could. They could change lives and improve
their communities, and we could support them in the effort.

Our faith groups, however, doubted our sincerity. And they had
every right to do so. For years, city government and religious groups
regarded each other suspiciously at best, downright antagonistically at
worst. I have written elsewhere that we took pains to gain their support
in three ways.[7] First, we formed an advisory council and spent time
talking with organizations before we announced the initiative, so that
there would be no surprises. Second, we looked for immediate and tangible ways to produce results and to demonstrate our sincerity, and we
only invited media attention when one of the organizations requested
it. And, as the requests for partnership and assistance grew, we tripled
the number of staff we had initially dedicated to work on the effort.

Our promise to local religious groups was not primarily financial.
We promised to help them accomplish the true community-building
work they were doing, whatever it was. This meant helping them navigate city hall's red tape, assisting them in getting funding from sources
to which they usually did not have access, and helping them build the
partnerships in the community that would give their mission its greatest impact. We did not assist them in proselytization or any directly religious instruction or worship. We did assist them in doing the good in the
community that their faith impelled them to do.

FPA forged alliances with more than 500 congregations and other
organizations in the Indianapolis area. It created a summer youth program partnership between the city and a variety of organizations that
served more than 4,000 Indianapolis youth. It provided assistance to
Indianapolis's largest teen abstinence program, which involved more
than 3,500 public- and private-school youth in a peer-mentoring
approach to abstinence. Altogether, it helped organizations provide programs that benefited more than 10,000 Indianapolis youth.

FPA facilitated partnerships between more than thirty churches
and twenty public schools. The partnerships provided tutoring, after-
school programming, and mentoring for the students. In an effort to
provide grassroots care for the appearance and safety of neighborhoods,

FPA coordinated an "Adopt-a-Block" program in which thirty churches adopted more than sixty city blocks. It created an arrangement in which nearly fifteen churches maintained thirty city parks.

Here is how I would break down the areas in which FPA has had a noticeable impact in Indianapolis:

**Community Asset Building**. FPA helped turn liabilities (vacant warehouses and fire stations, crack houses, and the like) into assets such as youth centers, drug-counseling centers, parks, and transitional housing. Five major projects of this sort—and there were others—were carried out in about eighteen months' time. Chapter One told of the vacated property that Reverend Sanders converted into a drug relapse prevention center and the crack alley that Pastor Jay Height converted into a city park. FPA also worked with Robinson Community African Methodist Episcopal Church and the Indianapolis Black Firefighters Association to secure vacant firehouses for each of them to run youth and family programs. All of these are marvelous examples of turning a liability into a community asset. They drove away the bad and replaced it with the good.

These cases represent FPA's unique approach. Government can sell its unused assets and reap some economic benefit, or it can invest these assets back into the community to produce increased social capital—and thus a strengthened social fabric built on trust and relationships through which opportunity is created. The former approach is usual and conventional. The latter was central to FPA's activity.

**Crime and Safety**. In early 1999, we launched the Indianapolis Ten Point Coalition, based on the successful model in Boston, where Reverend Eugene Rivers led pastors to the streets in an effort to reduce crime and create positive alternatives for young people. The pastors in Indianapolis patrol the streets during high-crime times, usually on weekend nights. Unlike police officers, whose primary job is enforcement, the pastors are charged with offering spiritual intervention and ministry to those in need.

The program arrived on the scene the night we announced it during a snowy blizzard. After the press conference, we walked the streets with the pastors to send a message to the gangs that the ministers had come out from behind their pulpits to reclaim the streets. It worked, because gang leaders called right away to find out if the pastors were "for real." The pastors proved that they were indeed for real, and immediately began seeking job opportunities for the young people they met on the street.

Elder David Coatie, a leader in the effort, said, "We're meeting kids out there that are saying, 'We don't want to be out here, but we don't know what else to do.' So we started finding them jobs, good jobs that paid some money." And Reverend Charles Harrison, the Ten Point Coalition chairman, reported that the gangs actually started referring young people to the pastors once the pastors had proved they could get the youth off the streets and into jobs.

The Coalition was a quick success. Just nine months after starting, homicides had fallen by 50 percent in two crime-ridden areas where the Coalition patrolled most heavily. Through a strategic partnership with Jump Start, a program that trains young people for road construction jobs, youth have come off the street and found themselves making more than $20 per hour working with road crews. One participant who left the streets and went through the program said, "This is not just a job. It's a career opportunity. Before I got here, you name it, I did it—lots of terrible stuff. But with the churches, the pastors, and Jump Start, my life has turned around. I have a future."

**New Community Relationships**. Our work to connect churches to other socially redeeming work paid off in a number of different ways. Partnerships formed between churches and other public and private organizations unlike anything the city had ever seen. In one case, a church collaborated with a shelter for domestic violence victims to provide transportation for the children as their mothers received needed help and recovery services. In another case, churches provided community counselors in a pilot project that targeted child abuse and neglect cases before they grew into emergencies.

I referred earlier to partnerships churches had with public schools. Churches make logical partners for schools, which have an abundance of children needing after-school programming, tutoring, and other forms of support. Lakeview Christian Center, a congregation with more than 1,500 members on the city's west side, partnered with a school whose students faced all the problems associated with poverty. Church volunteers not only provided tutoring but also worked directly with the school's social worker to identify students whose families needed food and other supplies, and they would meet the families' needs. They also worked with advanced students after school to give them continuing opportunities to learn, and they participated in the school's efforts to keep kids away from drugs by sponsoring events that sent alternative, positive messages.

Churches were creative in their partnerships. Northside New Era Baptist Church purchased school uniforms for the children in their partner elementary school. The school's principal reported a decrease in conflict between kids and even a rise in academic performance. While churches were engaging the schools, they were also mowing city parks. Together, they mowed nearly fifty acres of parks on contracts totaling more than $60,000 at any given time. Englewood Christian Church, which mowed fourteen parks and accounted for nearly a third of the contract totals, runs its own Community Development Corporation. It owns several properties and provides transitional housing for members of its congregation and community that are saving to purchase their own homes. It also provides job-placement services. The mowing contract allowed it to employ people to whom it was providing other services. The mowing became an extension of Englewood's already successful ministry.

**Enhanced Resources**. Although FPA did not focus on money, it did negotiate some assistance for community groups. In less than two years, FPA was responsible for bringing more than $750,000 to faith-based organizations across the city. Small amounts of city funding and the assistance of FPA's staff helped organizations attract outside funding. Most grassroots organizations of the size that participated in FPA cannot attract foundation grants. But with FPA as a partner, and with other partners which they would find through FPA, these organizations suddenly gained credibility with funders.

Beyond financial support, FPA was an important source of other valuable resources. FPA identified nonprofit organizations across the city that needed computers, and partnered with a church that would repair used computers before turning them over to the organizations. The church's pastor who oversaw the process described it this way: "We never would have thought of this kind of ministry before FPA approached us with the idea. We have even created a program in which we train teens in our community in computer assembly. Not only do they help prepare the computers for our program, we make a deal with them that if they can put together a computer that works by the end of their class, all by themselves, they get to keep it. Most of these kids come from homes where they don't have computers. I couldn't be happier with the way this has worked out." And not only has FPA turned the city's junk into someone else's fully functioning computer, it also began working with the city to take its discarded furniture to community organizations that needed chairs, desks, tables, and lamps.

Of course, one can never estimate the value of a mayor's bully pulpit for small, faith-based groups. We encouraged foundations, businesses, and individuals to take the faith community seriously and back their work financially. We put pressure on government agencies to stop ignoring faith-based organizations but to consider them as viable partners.

We never pressured congregations, however. FPA was, after all, on their side. And so, when FPA director Isaac Randolph stood behind a pulpit one Sunday morning at the invitation of Lakeview Christian Center, he merely described how he thought the church could actively involve itself in a neighborhood that needed lots of help just down the road from the church. The congregation took up an offering out of its own goodwill, however, and ended up collecting $112,000 with a commitment to begin community-redeeming work in the needy area.

Only a year after starting, FPA had a 25 percent name recognition among Indianapolis residents—more than most of our other programs. This was not a sign of slick marketing on our part. It was an indicator that the effort mattered to people. FPA continued to have opponents in the community. But frankly, we expected a lot more opposition when we started. This never happened, though, because all involved parties operated according to a high level of purpose and integrity. Religious liberty was protected. No one's rights were infringed. Tax dollars did not pay for any sectarian activity. But most of all, people were empowered to unleash the power of partnership in a way unseen before in our city's history.

Not only did FPA build an important bridge between city hall and religious organizations, it became a laboratory for learning. It revealed a number of valuable lessons about the complex and unique characteristics of public relationships with faith-based organizations. I will treat these lessons at greater length in Chapter Seven.

*Endnotes*

[1] Theda Skocpol, "How Americans Became Civic," *Civic Engagement in American Democracy*, eds. T. Skocpol and M. Fiorina (Washington, D.C.: Brookings Institution Press & Russell Sage Foundation, 1999), 69.

[2] Jeffrey M. Berry, "The Rise of Citizen Groups," *Ibid.*, 369.

[3] Quoted in Janet Reingold, Jennifer Wootton, and Andrew Hahn, *The Indy Story: Urban Systems Reform and Community Revitalization in Indianapolis During the Stephen Goldsmith Years (1992-1999)* (Washington, D.C.: The Annie E. Casey Foundation, 2000), 46.

[4] *To Empower People: From State to Civil Society*, Twentieth Anniversary Edition, ed. M. Novak (Washington, D.C.: AEI Press, 1996), 148.

[5] Daniel T. Oliver, "The National Assembly: Guarding Nonprofits' Government Funds," *Alternatives in Philanthropy* (Washington, D.C.: Capital Research Center, 1999).

[6] Theodore Roosevelt, *The Roosevelt Policy* (New York: The Current Literature Publishing Company, 1919), 28-29.

[7] See my essay titled the same as this section, "Having Faith in Our Neighborhoods: The Front Porch Alliance," in *What's God Got to Do with the American Experiment?*, eds. E. J. Dionne and John J. DiIulio (Washington, D.C.: Brookings Institution Press, 2000), 72-78.

# SECTION THREE
# The City and Citizenship Tomorrow

# Chapter Five

# Strengthening Communities

Our experience with encouraging grassroots citizenship in Indianapolis taught us two important, transferable lessons. While these might seem obvious, they are by no means the prevailing opinion in policies and programs aimed at empowering those left out of mainstream prosperity.

First, successful urban revitalization requires local empowerment. National policies, large programs, and big intentions may help set the tone for local empowerment efforts, but they are only as good as the organization and commitment of the local community.

Second, municipal citizenship is about building character that gets engaged. Empowerment occurs not merely by specifying certain economic or political outcomes in advance but by strengthening people's capacity for self-governance, involvement, and cooperation. If we only focus on improving the current financial condition of a certain group of people, for instance, we may have done too little to develop the values and skills needed to sustain them during economic slowdowns. Character that gets engaged is more than a propensity for volunteerism but a penchant for entrepreneurial creativity.

## Municipal Citizenship and the Importance of Locality

A surprising amount of agreement now exists on the value of local community-building initiatives. From police strategy to public-housing developments to job-training initiatives, there has been an emerging consensus that says success is dependent on the degree to which individuals who need assistance have more community-based choices.

Empowerment happens when real people in real communities gain more control over their destiny. It occurs when people have the wherewithal and resources to act on their ambitions and find satisfaction in the active pursuit of their well-being rather than the passive consumption of goods and services. Several years ago, a study funded by the Annie E. Casey and Rockefeller Foundations, together with the U.S. Department of Housing and Urban Development, argued that this consensus has been driven by much recent literature emphasizing "that the existence of networks of nongovernmental civic institutions is vital to the performance of *governance* at all levels. But more basically, it has reminded us how critical neighborhood level institutions (e.g., associations, churches) and friendship networks are to families and children everywhere."[1] The difference between recent community-based activity and that of the 1960s, the authors say, is that the former has been driven mainly by nongovernmental organizations (as opposed to the federal government's Model Cities and Community Action Programs) and has more to do with partnering and "self-help" opportunities than the "fighting city hall" typical of the 1960s.[2] Empowerment happens at the neighborhood level by organizations that know the neighborhood and its people.

In *Comeback Cities*, Paul Grogan and Tony Proscio reiterate this point with respect to the explosive growth of community development corporations (CDCs) in the past thirty years. "Most of today's actual CDCs," they write, "were formed long after the whole tumultuous 'community action' episode [of the 1960s and 1970s] was over, and many of them can scarcely imagine what all the fuss was about. They now make up a wide variety of citizen-formed self-help groups trying to revitalize their own neighborhoods or towns, in close league with local governments, businesses, churches, and other branches of the 'establishment' their predecessors had so reviled."[3]

Today's version of locally driven empowerment efforts are largely products of nongovernmental activity. They are remnants of the tendency of Americans to self-organize into associations to get things done for the community's good, which has been the hallmark of American civil society since its beginning. Any government effort, then, to empower residents cannot ignore this very important point. The government-driven community action of the Great Society years, in many ways, was more prone to replace rather than build on this tendency. It made community programs dependent on the federal government.

As policymakers and governments grow more interested in local initiatives, we would do well not to repeat this mistake. Government's role in local empowerment is to create an environment where self-organization is more likely than before, and in which residents find it worth their while to organize for their greater good. Its role is to give communities the security that their organization will not be in vain. It oversteps its role when it tells organizers what to do, how to do it, and then pays them to follow the steps of dependency.

The general agreement in America about the value of local initiatives is very encouraging. This late twentieth-century development succeeds nearly one hundred years of focusing on broad, national campaigns to solve problems. Progressivism, which began under Herbert Croly's leadership at the dawn of the twentieth century and continued in a variety of guises through the end of the century, was a well-intentioned effort aimed at orchestrating national solutions to problems. Localities were, in many cases, not dealing well with their problems. National answers eclipsed community-based problem solving.

As we move away from top-down, national-based solutions to locally driven community initiatives, we still have to deal with the large government institutions and processes created largely by national-based agendas. And these agendas still have their defenders. The newly developing tension is not so much between local and national layers of government, but between devolution by the federal government to state and local institutions, and funding and policies that allow more discretion by the person to whom the help is directed. The debate essentially pits a state or local professional bureaucrat to whom authority has been devolved against individual citizens who want to decide on their own, assisted by a voucher, where to receive assistance. The school reform debate exemplifies this issue, for example, in the case of whether neighborhood-based schools can perform at high levels absent parental choice.

"Municipal citizenship" as we use the term here is practically synonymous with "compassionate conservatism," which assumes that government acknowledges its public responsibility for certain goods such as food, shelter and medicine. However, it also assumes that an effective delivery system must both be decentralized to the community level and respect the individual choices of both those who wish to be helped and those who strive to assist.

## Municipal Citizenship and Can-Do Character

This point is equally important but enjoys less consensus than the generally accepted idea that empowerment has to be locally driven. I have used the term "value-shaping organizations" for a number of years as a more specific name for what are often now called "faith-based" or simply "community-based organizations." As I indicated earlier, the Front Porch Alliance was founded not only because community-based organizations could benefit from a closer working relationship with city hall, but also because they were specialists in positive human change.

Specifically, many organizations in neighborhoods promote the positive behavior that prevents social problems, and they are in a position to enforce what they promote. Their members ban together to confront drug dealers, tell kids to get off the street and then provide a place for them to go, and knock on the door of their neighbor or fellow parishioner to ask why he's not at work.

Value-shaping organizations promote traits that help people succeed at work and in the community. They also promote a can-do spirit in their neighborhood. In other words, they promote solid character and civic engagement. Wherever pockets of marketable and engaged character are found, dependency is usually low, entrepreneurial activity high, and people get things done. Any successful, government-initiated empowerment effort should build on this quality and help it grow.

If the Neighborhood Empowerment Initiative had merely turned organizations into passive consumers of public goods and services, or flooded them with resources without encouraging them to proactively take ownership of their communities, then it would have been little better than meaningless. If an empowerment effort engages people without helping them develop the kinds of skills that help them succeed as workers and citizens, it will likely promote dependency over time.

This point is more controversial than the first point about locality. I once heard a pastor complain that conservatives always want to turn "poverty into a character issue" and ignore other societal and systemic injustices. I agree with him that poverty concerns much more than the character of poor individuals and families. Municipal citizenship understood as building marketable and engaged character involves removing barriers so that using marketable talents and engaging oneself in the community seem like worthwhile things to do. It is not only about changing people's habits. It is about changing people's environment so that their ambitions and motivations can be fulfilled.

Many of the residents on the near-west side of Indianapolis care about marketable skills and character. They care about civic engagement. But they needed help making these qualities appealing to more people in their community. They needed to be given the tools and relationships and resources that would help them begin to persuade their neighbors that trying to transform their neighborhood would be worth it.

There must be a balance between individual character and government's responsibility to open up opportunity for people. Government has a responsibility to remove barriers that limit opportunity. It must take on discrimination and failing schools, and inadequate day care and transportation systems. But individuals and their community leaders must advocate the importance of work and responsibility. Without opportunity, the latter often appears pointless and, correspondingly, opportunity provides no real advantage when individuals do not have the character to pursue it rightly.

University of Pennsylvania's John DiIulio, former director of the White House Office of Faith-Based and Community Initiatives, speaks about "sacred places serving civic purposes." I like this phrase because value-shaping organizations—many of which are faith-based "sacred places"—serve to improve conditions that everyone cares about. A faith-based organization may want to help an addict kick his habit because of its belief that all people are made in God's image, and a county health official may want to help out of a concern for the community's overall quality of life—but both care about helping the addict overcome his drug dependency that has negative effects not only on him but, most likely, on his family and community. Both motivations serve "civic purposes."

Character that is engaged, as I have been discussing it here, serves two important civic purposes. If people improve their personal marketability, which is often just as much a matter of changing personal habits as learning technical skills, they will improve their economic condition over time. And if they become engaged in the life of their community, they will improve their social condition—and that of those around them—over time. In other words, they will improve the financial and social capital in their neighborhoods.

The question for us today, then, is this: if empowerment in our troubled neighborhoods depends on effective local action and invigorated value-shaping organizations, how do we—the heirs of Great Society's large institutions—respond? When consensus developed in the mid-1990s that it was better to help people get to work than to keep them on welfare, the welfare reform act was passed in 1996. With this act, the Great Society model of helping those left behind was proved outdated and ineffective, and states were given authority over helping people get into the workforce. Is this same kind of spirit, which animated welfare reform by simplifying and decentralizing, capable of changing the way we seek to empower our distressed neighborhoods?

## Public Challenges to Municipal Citizenship

Whenever people seem to agree easily that empowering troubled communities is a good thing, disagreement often immediately follows as specific strategies and tactics are discussed. The challenges facing successful municipal citizenship are great and the variety of interests many. Public initiatives need to diversify and expand the numbers of small service providers and other supportive organizations with which they work. Barriers that keep frontline community healers from participating need to come down, and mechanisms that engage them need to be implemented.

### Diverse Private Actors with Public Purposes

Repairing urban neighborhoods and restoring hope requires participation from multiple actors. Sometimes policy experts discuss urban reform as a national, state, or local matter, looking at it more in terms of devolution than anything else. The key to successful policy, in their minds, is the level occupied by the government ultimately in charge. Other experts see urban reform as a sectoral problem: the role of the public, private, and nonprofit sectors. Using empowerment tools to support urban neighborhoods calls for a range of responses and partnerships across all these dimensions. This multidimensional approach requires new concepts, programs, and management.

Federal policies that rely on devolution sometimes miss the fundamental need for restructuring governance in a way that fosters local decision-making across the sectors. Government resources need to be provided in a manner that facilitates grassroots decision-making and individual responsibility. But generally government does the opposite and maintains control of programs, many of which have cross purposes, produce incalculable inefficiency, and place confusing regulations on cities and communities. Much has been made over the years about multiple, conflicting federal programs, but it is worth noting that this multiplicity is felt at the level of community-based revitalization and citizenship.

Partnership governance suggests that the federal government funds important public goals in a way that allows local grassroots organizations to produce the results to fit the needs of the area and its people. Yet, creating more programs with more regulations makes this enormously difficult; in fact, it gives preference to large organizations that specialize in understanding government but are often less familiar with neighborhood dynamics. For example, consider the case of the federal government's involvement in local economic development. A recent General Accounting Office (GAO) report categorizes federal economic development into six general program categories, five of which had to do with the construction of business facilities or necessary infrastructure to support development. The sixth has to do with programs for planning economic growth strategies. The report identifies ten federal agencies and twenty-seven subagencies that administer seventy-three programs, all of which can be said to support one or more of the six program categories.[4] If the definition of "economic development programs" is expanded to include other activities such as small business and community development, the number of programs grows to nearly 350. This type of complexity requires a lot of "insider" know-how by organizations wishing to work with government. It also requires a high degree of public sector professionalism, even in the best devolutionary environment. Simple, flexible programs with clearly defined goals, on the other hand, lend themselves well to partnership governance and would allow a greater variety of participants to act as public partners.

### Encouraging Participation by Removing Barriers to Small, Effective Groups

One way to encourage more private local solutions would be to remove the barriers that prevent some of the best neighborhood organizations from even being able to compete for resources. New legislative and regulatory efforts would remove these barriers. I spoke with an excellent national organization that has hundreds of local chapters, Keep America Beautiful, after we had formed the partnership with them that I discussed earlier. I asked them if they used Americorps volunteers from the Corporation for National Service and was surprised when they said they did not. The reason? Their small national office could not provide enough assistance to the local chapters in responding to the paperwork and regulatory demands.

But paperwork barriers are only part of the problem. An agency may approve applications for funding from nontraditional providers, such as faith-based or small community centers, but then require the small organizations to fundamentally change the way they operate. I was shocked to find that my own employees were requiring faith-based organizations that received HUD grants to remove religious symbols from the walls. They informed me that HUD regulations required this. In other words, government would fund faith-based organizations only if they looked and acted like government.

Multiple programs inhibit customized solutions and greatly increase the compliance costs. So I was pleased in 1995 to publicly support HUD's ambitious "Reinvention Blueprint" before the Senate Subcommittee on Housing Opportunity and Community Development. The Blueprint, a project begun by former Secretary Henry Cisneros, aimed to eliminate scattershot programs and consolidate them into broader initiatives. It also aimed to reduce its staffing levels significantly. The perverse result, once Congress and the administration were finished with it, was more rules and fewer people to translate them and approve local requests. The staff reductions were easier to implement than large-scale programmatic reform. Community organizations are far too busy with the pressing needs of their neighbors to translate and comply with these myriad rules. And when they comply, they often have to configure their services to fit the federal program. To the extent that local community leaders and community officials are trying to make their neighborhoods more self-governing, they at least deserve to have the federal resources available to them be usable, accessible, and helpful. We waste their precious talents by making them spend inordinate amounts of time and resources on processes unrelated to finding solutions and getting things done.

Excessive procedural regulations limit one of the most important assets a city or any locality has: the knowledge of the particulars of a problem it is facing and thus the ability to customize solutions. In Indianapolis we formed a Regulatory Study Commission to help us identify the barriers that were keeping our citizens from promptly fixing problems, maintaining productivity in their work, or simply getting on with life in areas where no interference from government was necessary.

Between 1994 and 1999, the commission saved Indianapolis taxpayers $3.3 million by getting rid of 157,000 processes and regulations, an accomplishment for which *Investor's Business Daily* cited the city as a national leader. As far as I know, no one misses any of them. No one has been lost in confusion without the regulations to guide them. But even our own reform efforts did not free us up to serve our residents in a way they deserved, because federal and state regulations often bound us to procedures that were counterintuitive and unhelpful.

For example, as part of our empowerment efforts, we wanted to provide incentives for residents in one of our lower-income neighborhoods to invest in home repairs. I asked that funds from a particular HUD program be made available in a pilot project that would bring investment to 100 houses. City staff rejected the idea as impractical. It would be more practical to use only local funds, they said, because HUD regulations required that the older houses be brought up to existing codes. This curious result meant we could not help a senior citizen who possessed limited assets fix her roof or weatherize her house, which she could not afford without the assistance. So the roof continued to leak, further limiting her assets as her house value decreased.

In another case, HUD had foreclosed a scattered site housing project that it had helped construct years earlier. On behalf of a coalition of residents and community groups, I proposed that we demolish the units, give the residents vouchers, build lower density houses on the same property and on land that the city would donate. Top HUD officials agreed to the logic of the plan. It then took us more than two years to navigate through the regulatory maze standing in the way of what was, in reality, a commonsense idea.

Many families in distressed urban areas cannot get on the road to self-sufficiency without help. And many communities in those urban areas cannot be successfully empowered so long as the most sensible thing to do with the resources available is prevented by the rules attached to those resources.

### *Minimizing the Bureaucratic Professionalism That Inhibits Innovation and Good Sense*

There is a natural and ongoing clash between government officials, at all levels, who are subject matter experts (that is, they know everything about a particular public program) and local officials who lack detailed program knowledge but really understand the local conditions. It is naive to assume that all local leaders instantly can figure out the solutions to the tough problems they face, but it is equally unwise to assume that any professional, no matter how good, can apply a rule-driven solution to every community across the country or even within one city.

Accountability must accompany the use of public money. And it would seem logical therefore to ask bureaucrats to measure results, rather than to dwell on input and process details. Even this seemingly straightforward approach comes with serious obstacles. First the difficulty of measuring performance often justifies not even trying. In areas like social services, simply identifying what is a positive output or outcome is problematic. So, while one agency might be trying to create employment in a specific neighborhood, another might be bussing workers from the neighborhood to remote job sites. It is simply easier to continue working at cross-purposes. And, with some cities spending one-third of their budget complying with federal mandates and regulations, no one has time to try to articulate a common vision or goal for the people affected by the programming.

If our agencies would structure programs according to well-defined results, then the logical providers of program services would be the organizations that produce results. In many of our cities and communities, this means the small frontline organization such as the church or community center. Without a thoroughgoing commitment to real results, public managers have little incentive to do what is inconvenient. It is easier to contract with large organizations who may or may not know the community they are serving. It is inconvenient to break up contracts into a number of smaller grants so that a range of small organizations can participate. And yet, if we really want results, this may well be what our agencies at the state and local levels need to be forced to do.

Public resources foster local solutions best when the programs use market mechanisms. Market principles and practices, if we let them work, will lead us to the most effective local change-makers. Market mechanisms can exist at the macro level, using the tax code, or the

micro level, with vouchers going to the person in need. Both mechanisms operate more efficiently and effectively than grant programs.
They place the accountability for the success of a program on individual
citizens' choices in the case of vouchers. Vouchers change the role of the
public professional from the manager of program details to a coordinator of related activity and a dispenser of information needed for citizens
to make informed decisions.

Tax credits use market mechanisms, create less opportunity for
waste, fraud, and abuse inside the programs (although they still present
temptation at the point of application), and allow more easily the mixing
of nonpublic money. The advantage of tax credits is that they require
very little results oversight. For example, the federal government provides substantial benefits to low-income families through a work-based
tax credit, the Earned Income Tax Credit (EITC), rather than a welfare
check. Vouchers and tax credits[5] enable people to select the best means
to resolve whatever problems they are facing and facilitate a diverse supply of providers. Opponents of market mechanisms are often representatives of existing providers or interest groups whose authority or
position is challenged. The opponents' biggest problem, however, is that
they underestimate the ability of voucher or tax-credit recipients to
make good choices. Americans are waking up to the falsity of this
assumption. Recent years have revealed the willingness of a wide variety
of common-minded Americans to support market mechanisms in education through the charter school and voucher movements. And the fact
that some Americans need someone to make choices for them, because
of their disabilities, is insufficient reason to deprive the rest of having
the ability to have more information, authority, and control.

Community-based citizenship is an asset that can overcome some
liabilities. Yet, economic revitalization has suffered from two related
problems. It has failed to use market-based tools to stimulate the buying power, labor pool, and other assets of the inner-city community; and
it has developed cumbersome tools often accompanied by top-down prescriptive solutions. The disincentives to invest in cities are many: taxes,
crime, poor infrastructure, regulations, inferior education. Each has its
own answer, and cities have been finding answers. No doubt some government intervention is necessary. One straightforward way to reduce
these structural imbalances is to provide tax incentives or at least
reduce tax inequities that hinder investment in our urban areas. A
reduction in the taxes that cities pay would result in increased investment in them. This is not only a matter of cutting federal taxes: many
cities and states would do well to examine how they levy their own
taxes. But without federal tax relief, local tax reform will usually be
unlikely to achieve its desired impact.

New York City, for example, pays more in federal taxes than it receives in returned investment, and the tax burden it places on its residents and businesses is 79 percent higher than those of the next nine largest U.S. cities. When the city cut its hotel tax rate several years ago, tax revenues from tourism rose significantly, aided in part by the city's tough stance on crime that made New York an appealing destination. What would happen if New York, or any city, relinquished a variety of federal urban-aid programs in exchange for a reduction in federal taxes? We watched Indianapolis residents send much more money to the state coffers than the city received back in assistance from the state. What might happen at the state level if a city were to have its state taxes reduced or eliminated on the same grounds?

In an insightful article, Nicolas Lemann points out that over the past thirty years, community development programs such as Empowerment Zones have consistently under-performed expectations. And, a number of original proponents of such programs do not show continued enthusiasm for them. Lemann wonders about our targeted strategies for revitalizing urban areas: "Administration after Administration has pondered the ghettos and then settled on the idea of trying to revitalize them economically—even though there is almost no evidence that this can work."[6] But the correct question is *how* these programs have conceived of economic revitalization.

Even some tax-credit incentives come with very burdensome and prescriptive federal requirements in how those incentives can be used. They look more like social programs than credits in the way they distribute money for everything from neighborhood cleanup to senior, youth, and child care programs. And a variety of highly targeted tax credits for employers have proven to be largely ineffective. There has been the Targeted Jobs Tax Credit (TJTC), which was replaced by the Work Opportunity Tax Credit. Then the Welfare to Work Tax Credit came on the scene. During the Clinton administration, the Department of Labor found these credits to be ineffective in improving the incomes of the beneficiaries.

Programs such as these, typical of empowerment zones, arrive with very detailed prescriptions, making them more like mandates than markets. They require more political lobbying than they do business plans. They ignore the importance of the competitive edge that inner cities possess, as Harvard business professor Michael Porter has pointed out. Programs aimed particularly at low-income, urban areas should be realistic in the way they try to attract investment. While it is too soon to tell, perhaps the funding of the recently initiated by New Market Tax Credits may prove successful. Like the Low Income Housing Tax Credit, which attracts investment in rental housing, New Market Tax Credits

attract investment for commercial real estate and business development. They are allocated by the Treasury Department rather than the
states or HUD, and they work solely through "community development
entities," which could be a nonprofit that sets up a limited partnership
or a limited liability company to attract investors. The credits are based
on the equity investment, not underlying assets, and are thus more
modest than if they were used to pay for buildings, for example.

Of course, grants for particular programs will need to continue, particularly those that heighten the ability of low-income urban residents to
advance in careers. This would include a range of services such as on-the-
job training, child-care assistance, debt counseling, transportation assistance, and so on. This takes us to another important point, namely that
we need to encourage innovation at the local level through our policies.

If we are going to convert more targeted programs to block grants,
then priorities need to be set in a way that encourages the movement of
authority down to the lowest level possible. Federal welfare reform made
employment for welfare recipients the chief priority and then gave states
block grants with maximum flexibility to get the job done. The block-
grant structure has encouraged the involvement of new grassroots
groups, including small faith-based organizations, as states have turned
toward localities for help in getting people into productive employment.
Moving from welfare to work requires a complex set of services that can
only be provided by the surrounding community. The former cash-assistance welfare system required nothing of localities, but by prioritizing
employment, the new policy has required states to do something that
they cannot do without active local employment support networks.

Aside from block grants, we should review policies that make payments directly to individuals to make sure they cohere with other dollars that flow into communities with the aim of improving them.
Between 1978 and 1998, federal payments to individuals rose from 31.8
percent to 62.5 percent. There is nothing inherently wrong with this,
and in many cases, it is better for families to receive certain benefits
such as food stamps and different kinds of vouchers directly. Certainly,
the old welfare system made direct payments to individuals on the condition that they not work, which was generally harmful.

Welfare reform changed this. It coheres nicely with the EITC by
moving people into the work environment where the EITC is "waiting"
for them, so to speak. Child care in many areas is now voucherized,
allowing working parents to choose the child care situation that fits
their work life. A recent Brookings Institution report makes clear that
the general effects of welfare reform have been positive on low-income
women and children: earnings among a substantial number of low-
income, female-headed households are up, and child poverty has

decreased.[7] Making various forms of assistance cohere around the right set of core principles—in this case, the value of work—has its payoffs.

## Municipal Citizenship and Subsidiarity

I have already argued that the best solutions to social problems come when people start working together through local organizations. In the first couple of chapters, I laid out some general guiding principles by which we tried to turn this argument into action in Indianapolis. We operated with the belief that local residents know best when given good information, that they need additional resources and training, that high standards must be expected of all stakeholders, and that government must offer residents security by providing public goods and services. These principles were the framework in which our relationships with neighborhood organizations were formed.

They were also the principles that supported an approach that we preferred to devolution, what the Europeans call subsidiarity. It essentially denotes political organizations in which policies and decisions are made at the lowest possible level of governance. Of course, we never used the word *subsidiarity,* which would likely have only confused people and probably scared away potential allies. But we learned that enthusiasm for local forms of authority does not necessarily translate into effective action without an understanding of subsidiarity. For all the excitement we currently see in America for "community-building," "devolution," and other expressions of confidence in local governance, we will fall short of our aspirations if we—and urban leaders, especially—do not think through how to truly invest decision-making authority into communities and neighborhoods.

Washington has a responsibility to help those whom prosperity has left behind. But it needs to help in a way that respects both the individuals who need help and the community around them, which is best positioned to provide the help. This requires a strong combination of policies that gives localities both the freedom and the responsibility that come with decision-making authority. Principled block grants that drive authority down to counties and cities, tax credits and vouchers that maximize individual choice, and an overall tax policy that fosters economic opportunity—all of these create an environment likelier to empower small, community-based organizations to lead the way in strengthening their communities by improving the lives around them.

## Endnotes

[1] G. Thomas Kingsley, Joseph B. McNeely, and James O. Gibson, "Community Building Coming of Age" (Washington, D.C.: Urban Institute, 1997), 5.

[2] *Ibid.*, 5-6.

[3] Paul Grogan and Tony Proscio, *Comeback Cities: A Blueprint for Urban Neighborhood Revival* (Boulder, Colorado: Westview Press, 2000), 67.

[4] "Economic Development: Multiple Federal Programs Fund Similar Economic Development," U.S. General Accounting Office (September 2000): 5.

[5] A refundable tax credit, i.e. one that pays out to the recipient regardless of whether he or she has paid the requisite taxes, is essentially a voucher, depending on the timeliness and frequency of the payment.

[6] Nicolas Lemann, "The Myth of Community Development," *The New York Times Magazine* (January 9, 1994): 28.

[7] Ron Haskins, Isabel Sawhill, and Kent Weaver, "Welfare Reform: An Overview of Effects to Date," Policy Brief No. 1, The Brookings Institution (January 2001).

# Chapter Six

# Investing in Social Capital and Value-Enhancing Partnerships

Washington can get regulations out of the way of community empowerment initiatives. And it can take new steps to make sure that innovation, rather than abuse, results from removing them. But even in its most innovative, well-funded programs, it can never do the work of municipal citizenship. That happens on the ground as greater numbers of citizens gain more control over the future of their communities.

## Social Capital and Values

By promoting local voluntary organizations in Indianapolis, we tried to provide the context for people to experience community in a problem-solving environment. This encouraged people to rely on their commitment to shared values to get things done, and it resulted in the production of social capital. Neighborhood organizations help people share wins, losses, praise, and blame—all of which are needed to build a culture that values accomplishment and provides comfort amidst failure.

As citizens involve themselves in neighborhood groups, they take on more responsibility for setting agendas, executing projects, and running programs. They acquire a sense of shared ownership for the community. A shared commitment is necessary for a community to produce results that last.

Government can and should play a role in revitalizing our communities, but it can only do so by supporting, not supplanting, the institutions that nurture virtue and inspire positive action. Small, local, neighborhood-based organizations that are serving community needs deserve government's support, since it is primarily through their efforts that communities will be renewed. The future of social capital depends on them. For this reason, public officials and community leaders are especially smart to encourage municipal citizenship beyond its pragmatic form alone, but also its social capital and value-enhancing forms.

Social capital generates an incentive for neighbors to participate in their communities and helps reinforce positive norms. It is clear that government alone cannot create virtuous cities, but knowing this does not tell us what to do about declining levels of social capital. By most measures, ties to each other and the places where we live have been slipping. According to Robert Putnam, over the past several decades,

- Parents having dinner with their children has declined by about one-third.
- Parental involvement in their children's school is down about one-third.
- Attendance at local community meetings is down about 50 percent.
- Experience working for a local party or other political organization is down about 60 percent.
- Voting is down about 25 percent.
- Neighbors spending a social evening with other neighbors is down about 20 to 25 percent.
- Trust for others in daily life (such as neighbors, store clerks, and so on) is down about 40 percent.
- Having friends over to one's house is down about 30 to 40 percent.
- Working on community projects is down about 40 percent.[1]

These figures are indicative of a widespread decline in social capital across all socioeconomic strata in America. Urban areas in which economic opportunity is low and crime is high have been hardest hit by declining social capital over the past thirty years. The effects of declining trust and interconnectedness are starker, and the options for dealing with less social capital are fewer. Replenishing social capital in these areas requires strengthening the institutions that can reinforce positive norms and foster promising relationships among residents and other institutions. The important contribution of religious organizations to social capital is discussed in the next chapter.

To take social capital seriously is to realize that so-called innovative policies may be miserable failures if they are viewed as elixirs that can be ingested by a community without investing in relationships. And relationships are not exactly the same thing as partnerships. There is much enthusiasm about partnerships today, and a good bit of it is justified. Many foundations require that organizations partner together as a condition for receiving funding. More and more local governments are trying to foster partnerships to solve a range of problems. To the extent that partnerships raise organizational capacity or heighten problem-solving ability by putting knowledge from separate organizations to work in a collective effort, partnering makes sense.

But the kinds of relationships that generate social capital are as much between people as organizations. These kinds of relationships require high levels of trust to get things done. They require not just that the police department and neighborhood organizations get together to carry out community policing. Rather, they require that police *officers* and neighborhood *residents* come together as a team that works together, not merely as representatives of the interests of different organizations—though they are that as well.

On the near-west side of Indianapolis neighbors trusted police enough to help quell potential disturbances after well-intentioned but aggressive police actions; but they also expected police officials to respond to complaints about inappropriate police conduct. This can only happen where there is trust. Trust involves the confidence that each party is responsive to the other's concerns and interests.

While fostering social capital requires diverse approaches to building relationships, values, and networks, I see two main areas where city leaders should concentrate activity.

> *First, invest in the creation of citywide social-capital generating, value-enhancing initiatives—such as the Front Porch Alliance—as a way of bolstering human services and other community-building programs.*

Again, programs by themselves are as strong as the relationships in the community. Public and private officials need to consider specific projects that address particular needs, such as mentoring, as a piece of a larger puzzle, such as lagging test scores or fatherlessness or after-school programming. We looked at partnerships with faith-based groups not merely as a way to address a particular problem, but rather as a way to extend the reach, and social cohesion, of a variety of publicly beneficial initiatives. Youths enrolled in a job-training program or park cleanup activity or a peer-mentoring program at a strong neighborhood organization, we hoped, would be more likely to develop a sustained relationship with the organization. The more people a church helped, for instance, the more respect and social capital the church would develop in its neighborhood and the greater the chance that the church would be viewed by other organizations in the community as a viable partner for future initiatives.

The full strength of frontline change agents will be realized through a wide range of activities. Crack houses need closing down. Families need transitional housing amidst a caring community. People in job training may need debt counseling. Noncustodial fathers often need employment and reconciliation with their children in a safe and neutral environment. Families need child care close to home or work. The list goes on, and value-shaping organizations can play a role in all of these areas. The more they are active across a broad range of initiatives, the healthier the relationships in the community will be.

As a part of this effort, urban entrepreneurs would do well to cultivate relationships with a wide variety of local intermediary organizations to help facilitate the devolution of programs to community-based organizations. Local intermediaries can coordinate smaller value-shaping organizations around initiatives, and they can serve to pass funds to smaller organizations that are typically not on the radar screens of large public and private funding sources.

Intermediaries are valuable "matchmakers" at both the horizontal and vertical levels. They connect grassroots organizations together by bringing them together for common projects. They also connect organizations "on the ground" with the larger institutions such as public agencies, foundations, and even corporations. An intermediary may be a community development corporation, a YMCA, a Goodwill Industries operation, the local United Way, or a nonprofit formed exclusively to serve this function.

The small neighborhood organization is a better source of social capital than even a citywide organization, but often its capacity for service does not match its heart. One way to solve the professionalism anxieties of bureaucrats is to match skilled providers with the outreach efforts of smaller players. For example, we found that Goodwill was better at job training for people facing multiple employment obstacles, but the neighborhood churches were a better source of access and support. In cases such as these, neighborhood-based organizations serve as referral sources and personal support mechanisms (through mentoring, counseling, day care, and so on), which only strengthens the training that the large organization is doing.

In general community-based, value-based organizations contribute significantly to social capital. Many grassroots organizations are based on relationships. Relationships are often their strongest asset, their strongest form of capital. Many of them provide services to people in their communities through the efforts of volunteers—even if they do not have much financial capital. Broadening their networks by hooking them up with additional resources and partners only spreads a spirit of cooperation and mutual assistance through a community. It also expands the range of opportunities, economic and otherwise, for the people those organizations serve. In other words, it helps create social capital in a community.

> *Second, invest in community-based employment networks, which provide both economic opportunity and networks of supportive relationships.*

Philip Kasinitz and Jan Rosenberg write, "Enterprise zone programs, by focusing on the location of jobs rather than the formation of social networks, fail to address the central problem" of urban underemployment. These programs, they argue, are not connected to what may be more promising, namely the creation of "proxy networks that can inform, socialize, and vouch for employees in much the same way that informal social and ethnic networks do now."[2] While the programs about which Kasinitz and Rosenberg write have had a chance to mature since they wrote these words, not much attention has been given to what they refer to as "proxy networks."

The Workforce Investment Act of 1998 was a step in this direction. It brought together many different federal funding streams under one umbrella and required states to form local boards consisting of at least half business sector representation. This legislation has motivated some local public officials and businesspeople to begin working together to form one-stop centers where multiple job-training services can be accessed at one time. It has also made them take customer satisfaction more seriously than in the past.

All of this is good, but federal legislation cannot create the "proxy networks" that many low-skilled and low-income workers need. Only imaginative local leaders can. At-risk families need a friendly face at a community center, but they often need more. They may need debt counseling that a local faith-based organization provides and a support group run by a neighborhood association. They will undoubtedly need employers that understand how to provide nontraditional human resources services that tap community networks.

Thankfully, our current federal legislation does not discourage forming relationships with multiple community partners—in fact, it encourages this now more than ever—but it does not make this happen of itself. Forming relationships that inspire at-risk individuals to look not just for a job but a career, that bring the best of business and the best of nonprofit services together, that mobilize neighborhood organizations to help create a culture of work in the community—these things are the soul that animate any public effort to confront joblessness and underemployment.

Together, community networks of value-based organizations and employment services can do a lot to build social capital. And when social capital increases, so do the quality and quantity of opportunities for people. The bar on commonly held standards gets raised.

*Third, adapt government operations to the nature of social capital and shared values rather than vice versa.*

We have begun to vigorously encourage community empowerment through our federal policies, however, without also encouraging urban leaders and officials to rethink their approach to community organizations. Our policies presuppose a certain level of sophistication in local organization that is often left unarticulated or unexplored.

There are a few things that any city administration should attempt to do on this front.

First of all, city officials should consider neighborhood organizations a regular part of "the public square" and treat them accordingly. The combination of professionalism and specialization leads officials to ignore neighborhood leaders until late in the game when it is time to convince them of the correctness of the city's initiative. Yet, if these indigenous leaders are involved in an ongoing and iterative process, they will add value. They will think of ways to involve and rally their neighbors that are beyond the capability of public professionals.

Before our code-compliance reforms, which I described earlier, neighbors battled us for years on code enforcement, which was an agonizingly inefficient process of complaining about a neighborhood eyesore. Citizens would complain about improper zoning, or a single-family residence made into a multifamily crack house, or towed cars littering the front yard of what appeared to be a repair station. They would get slowed down by single-minded public professionals who felt no urgency to move the process along. Once our reforms put the citizens in the driver's seat, the neighborhood coordinator would work with a team of people from different departments and agencies to respond to citizen complaints.

However they accomplish it, leaders in a city need to be intentional and clear about standards in the way they go about creating an official relationship with neighborhood organizations. As much as public officials may want to empower neighborhoods, they need to guard against corruption and mismanagement. I recently spoke with the mayor of a relatively large U.S. city who was trying to figure out how to devolve key responsibilities to community-based organizations that were either severely inept or corrupt or both. Like many mayors, this mayor had seen firsthand that the often-idealized view, "local knowledge is the best knowledge," can lead to abuse. City officials need to have their eyes wide open as they try to increase the participation of neighborhood organizations in the public process.

Any relationship with community organizations needs to be based on a clearly understood articulation of accountability and the values necessary for success. The belief that community-based organizations are a panacea for social ills and can thereby be exempt from basic standards of performance will only produce more, or different, social ills. By creating an official relationship between a city administration and community organizations, local leaders can build standards of accountability into the relationship that are easier to enforce than when no official relationship exists. Social capital, like anything else, needs to be called to its highest and best form by standards that keep the public good in clear view.

## Municipal Citizens

In the end, strengthening social capital and identifying shared values strengthens grassroots citizenship. Communities create citizens, and citizens create communities. This is the great complexity facing anyone who cares about crafting a more robust civil society. Where do you start? With communities? Citizens? Jean Bethke Elshtain, an insightful commentator on the nature of American democratic life, writes, "Civil society isn't so much about problem solving as about citizen and neighbor creating. Then and only then will we work together on other desired ends."[3] Civil society, as Elshtain implies, is often called on to develop all kinds of solutions that government and the market seem incapable of providing. But its chief aim is making citizens. And it does this by helping citizens take greater responsibility for their communities and by making communities more receptive to the efforts of citizens. In reality, if it is working well, civil society is solving problems by making citizens—all at the same time.

In Indianapolis, as I have explained in this book, we worked primarily through grassroots organizations to build citizens and communities. There are other ways, I am sure, but these organizations help accomplish a few important things related to citizenship.

For one thing, they provide the context for people to experience community in a problem-solving environment. This usually has the side effect of generating social capital. So, while citizens are united in a problem-solving effort, citizenship and community are strengthening one another at the same time.

Neighborhood organizations also help people share wins and losses, praise and blame—all of which are needed to build a culture that values accomplishment and provides comfort amidst failure. The more citizens are involved in neighborhood groups, and the more responsibility those groups assume for executing projects and running programs, the less those citizens will point across the usual "us-them" divide to city officials when the neighborhood experiences problems. A sense of shared ownership for a community is necessary for that community to produce results.

Peter Drucker has pointed out that cities historically are places that have offered freedom from the tight, coercive atmosphere of small towns and rural communities. He has also said that if "there are no communities available for constructive ends, there will be destructive, murderous communities—the gangs of Victorian England, or the gangs that today threaten the very social fabric of the large American city (and increasingly of every large city in the world)."[4] Certainly urban gangs often provide a cohesiveness for youths looking for structure and security in their lives—albeit a very negative and violent cohesiveness.

The challenge, then, is to find a way to live with the dynamic and transient nature of cities while working with those forms of cohesiveness and continuity that are available. If we hope for the kind of community one finds in a rural town, where everyone knows everyone else, and everyone seems to have time to stand outside the soda shop to talk about the town's goings-on, we will be disappointed. Cities just work differently. Drucker goes on to say that the nongovernmental, social sector organizations, such as the neighborhood groups, are the key to building community. And in a city, that certainly makes sense.

Organizations are formed to deal with community issues and problems, and in the process they may attract certain groups of citizens for one set of issues and have to work with other groups on other issues. And they have to be able to deal with the fact that their people may find work across town and move. The nature of the city provides disruption. Neighborhood organizations can mitigate the effects of this disruption, even though they cannot make it go away.

We also learned that civic engagement is only secondarily about "feeling at home" or "experiencing a sense of community." Much of the literature in America today by writers with communitarian sympathies longs for a restored sense of belonging among the people of America. But many of our urban residents do not have time to be communitarians.

They have serious problems to fix. They need time to repair their sagging front porches before they can commune with their neighbors on them. Civic engagement, we learned, is about organizing citizens around issues they care about. This must be done with an eye toward building strategic relationships between them and other organizations and among them as neighbors so that, as I said earlier, the task of problem solving will go hand-in-hand with citizen building. In other words, though the roles of fellowship and mutual good feeling are important to civic health, the process of developing citizens is really about people getting stuff done together.

Another important lesson we learned was that standards and accountability are not "tacked on" to community building: they are essential to it. Expectations need to be met, standards upheld, and accountability enforced. This is important for people to have dignity in what they do, and it also makes citizenship matter. So-called empowerment that is only about acting out of guilt or "helping" people by giving them resources without expectations is an insult to those it ostensibly helps. We found that residents who were the most serious about community building were as committed—if not more—to high standards as we were in city hall.

And finally, we learned that the most effective leadership style in communities is one that combines a commitment to improving the overall condition of a neighborhood with a servant-like willingness to help others. The popular business management author Jim Collins has found these traits combined in the highest-performing Fortune 500 CEOs. In his research he has discovered that the most successful CEOs combine a "hedgehog-like" commitment to a company vision with a humility that assumes responsibilities for poor performance and gives credit to others amidst success.

In the neighborhoods we worked with, these same traits held true with grassroots leaders. We watched as Olgen Williams championed the cause of the near-west side and attracted resources because of his vision. And we also saw him labor days and nights at his community center, comforting young kids that had nowhere to turn and offering his resources to others in the community. We watched Reverend Frank Alexander, a pastor in the Martindale-Brightwood community on the city's near northeast side, organize other pastors to form the Community Resurrection Partnership. He runs affordable housing initiatives out of his church, provides job training, and champions the role of the church in solving Indianapolis's problems. And yet no one will meet a more humble man. He always graciously gives credit to others while shying away from the accolades others give him. Almost anywhere you find successful community building occurring in cities across the nation, you will find leaders like these.

If we are to successfully bring empowerment to our cities—in short, if citizens are to build communities and communities to build citizens—then we need to have high, but realistic, aspirations for our neighborhood organizations. And we also need to find leaders that can see high enough to meet the aspirations and low enough to serve their fellow citizens.

## *Endnotes*

[1] Robert Putnam, *Bowling Alone*, 41 et al.

[2] Philip Kasinitz and Jan Rosenberg, "Why Enterprise Zones Will Not Work," *City Journal*, vol. 3, no. 4 (1993).

[3] Jean Bethke Elshtain, "Not a Cure-all," in *Community Works: The Revival of Civil Society in America*, ed., E. J. Dionne, (Washington, D.C.: Brookings Institution, 1998), 27.

[4] Peter Drucker, "Civilizing the City," *Leader to Leader*, no. 7 (Winter 1998), at http://www.pfdf.org/leaderbooks/L2L/winter98/toc.html.

# Chapter Seven

# Civil Society's New Challenge

*Public Sector Management and*
*Faith-Based Organizations*

## The Unique Contribution of Faith-Based Organizations

When in January 2001 President Bush set up the White House Office of Faith-Based and Community Initiatives, its charge was clearly represented in its name: to improve government's relationship with small, frontline faith and community-based organizations. The very purposeful decision to establish such an office was itself an acknowledgment that government imposes obstacles—sometimes intentionally and sometimes unintentionally—that preclude many neighborhood groups from receiving government support.

Large national organizations, including well-known faith-based groups such as the Salvation Army, Catholic Charities, Lutheran Services of America and the Association of Jewish Family and Children's Agencies, have long developed a successful track record of using public dollars to carry out their efforts. These national organizations bring the technical know-how that size and specialization provide.

Yet there is something special about small community groups, whether secular or religious. They bring grassroots knowledge of their community and nearby residents to the social services equation.

Whatever they may lack in administrative capacity and specialization is often compensated by their proximity to people they serve, their credibility in their neighborhood, and their sense of mission.

In this book I have described our efforts in Indianapolis to strengthen these groups, whether they were neighborhood associations or community development corporations. In Chapter Four, I described our particular outreach to faith-based organizations, and in the last chapter, I pointed to religious organizations as incubators of social capital and values. This chapter explores in greater depth the unique characteristics and challenges associated with public partnerships with local faith-based organizations, especially those known as the "little guy"—congregations usually run on a shoestring and frequently led by a part-time pastor.

The current national interest in small, primarily faith-based, solutions to social problems warrants an ongoing analysis of the experiences of faith-based groups that have partnered with government. During my twenty years as a public official in Indianapolis, faith-based efforts made a real and substantive contribution to the mix of solutions to our city's problems. As my experience with faith-based organizations evolved and matured, so did my views of the nature of their contribution to the public square. And my visits to other cities around the country that have successfully engaged faith-based organizations have confirmed and enlarged my views.

Today, given a growing national interest in faith-based organizations, it is important to understand what makes them unique and how public officials can best work with them. There is currently much talk about whether or not religious groups are better than secular organizations in providing services. Comparative studies need to be done on this front, for sure, but we also need to take account not only of who is doing what better, but what makes groups different from one another. What kinds of things do grassroots, faith-based organizations do that set them apart from other kinds of organizations?

Faith-based organizations take several approaches to engaging the surrounding community and partnering with government. I summarize these as follows: the pragmatic, the social capital, the moral/spiritual, and the accountability approaches. These approaches follow the types of municipal citizenship spelled out at the end of Chapter One. In this chapter, however, because of the unique character of faith-based organizations, I have broken down value-enhancing engagement into moral/spiritual and accountability approaches to community engagement.

### *The Pragmatic Approach*

During my time as prosecutor in Indianapolis, it was standard practice to incarcerate young offenders rather than find a suitable alternative, even for the nonviolent. There were simply insufficient placement opportunities in community service and other kinds of programs.

So I approached a friend, Pastor Tom Brown, of the Ebenezer Baptist Church, whose father had been very active in national and local civil rights efforts, and I asked him if he thought a group of inner-city churches would accept responsibility for placement of nonviolent young offenders. I explained the requirements: to make sure the young offenders discharged their responsibilities, went to school, performed community work, and stayed in counseling that was to be provided by the church.

In return, his response was equally pragmatic. He said he would be very interested in helping and could put together a network of pastors and a program to help. But he clearly stated that his church would need funding, not for the work with the probationers, but for training and assistance with respect to the reporting and paperwork that would be involved.

I was simply asking for help in a cause of mutual concern. We both wanted to help troubled young men succeed and stay out of prison. In any large city there are too many children facing too many troubles—often with far too few organizations actively helping. Pastor Brown and I were trying to take a straightforward approach to a problem. We were not trying to design or prove some larger ideological point about church-and-state issues. We both had an interest in helping young offenders. We each had something that could benefit the other.

The situation is the same in many cities and states across the country. Many local and state officials find their way to supporting faith-based solutions through the promise and efficacy of these groups and because existing alternatives are insufficient. The poorest or worst-off residents of a community deserve an opportunity to succeed in life, and if a religious organization can provide that opportunity better than anyone else, it makes perfect pragmatic sense to work with them.

### The Social Capital Approach

Declines in social capital are not helped by the general aversion to religion and religious institutions perpetuated by government and even large corporations. Every day, faith-based organizations across America undertake extraordinary efforts to improve their communities and the lives of troubled individuals. The contributions they make are, or should be, of interest to governments that also care about positive change and companies that want to make communities good for business.

If we care about social capital, we have to care about religion. Of the $203.5 billion given to charitable causes in America in the year

2000, 36.5 percent, or $74.3 billion, was given to houses of worship. If giving estimates are adjusted to remove individual giving to foundations, then religious giving increases to 43.4 percent of all giving. This is more than Americans give to anything else, whether it is education (13.8 percent) or the arts (5.7 percent) or the environment (3 percent) or whatever.[1]

Americans who attend religious services give, on average, 2.3 percent of their household income, compared to the 1.3 percent given by those who do not attend. And 76 percent of Americans who attend religious services volunteer, compared to the 55.5 percent national average.[2] Some surveys estimate that more than 90 percent of congregations offer social services. The social capital that is created and the civic purposes served by America's religious communities is almost impossible to fully estimate or appreciate.

This becomes highly important in urban revitalization efforts. Mayors tend to think in geographic terms. I was determined through our Building Better Neighborhoods initiative to improve the quality of life in eight of the city's most difficult communities. When I asked our city planners to plot the assets of those neighborhoods on a map, the most frequent assets turned out to be churches, with small businesses and community groups or centers also appearing. Along with strong leadership and confidence in the future, stabilizing an area requires a tangible beacon of hope around which people can rally. Faith-based organizations are that beacon: they can send a message that a neighborhood is worth living in and worth revitalizing.

Thus it seemed only logical that we should take very poorly maintained neighborhood or "pocket" parks and offer a small contract to neighborhood churches to maintain them. The churches recruited volunteers to care for the parks and proclaimed: these parks are not just impersonal city areas, but our area. The churches helped create a sense of ownership for the parks among residents, ensured safety, and promoted the use of the parks. More important than the actual work, however, was the strengthened community leadership position the faith-based organizations enjoyed. Their activism for park upkeep and safety sent the message that they were willing community partners, which created new relationships and higher levels of social capital for them.

This increased social capital in turn benefits the members and clients of faith-based and neighborhood associations. We saw this, for instance, in our effort to make summer job-training money available to neighborhood and faith-based groups so that they could develop programs. Not-for-profit organizations associated with neighborhood-based groups and congregations to provide a sense of vocational and life purpose to young men and women in the area.

Faith-based organizations provide not only a service but a community of care and support. They do not want a client to feel like he or she is just getting job training: they want the client to feel a part of a trusting community that just so happens to express its care by helping him or her find and keep a job. There is a big difference between this kind of approach and a standard service delivery program, however "community-based" it may claim to be.

Strengthening a community asset by leveraging its relationships with other groups and individuals is simply better for people who need help. Olgen Williams, perhaps Indianapolis's most successful neighborhood reformer, creates partnerships with the city and both religious and secular service providers. He then makes sure those partnerships turn into relationships for the people his organization serves. As he says,

> What it really comes down to is that are we creating relationships. Because in those relationships you deal with heart issues, those lifestyle issues. As long as a person is just a program recipient, a program client, that won't happen. If I don't have a relationship with you, I don't have the ability to begin to hold you accountable and begin to deal with those tough issues.

Another form of social capital that faith organizations produce is what Harvard's Bob Putnam calls bridging social capital: the social capital that brings disparate groups together.[3] Thus we encouraged, albeit without enormous success, partnerships between suburban and urban congregations. As wealthier and even many middle-class families moved out from the heart of the city over several decades, it became impossible for them to understand the context in which many urban families lived. Many commentators express alarm about the absence of positive role models in many urban areas, which is no doubt a very real concern, but I was also concerned about the effect of urban exoduses on suburban residents. The tough underside of the city was out of their sight and mind. They were shielded from all that they do not like about the city while benefiting from their proximity to it. I thought that if they could begin to help those left behind, we might begin to see a new bridge built across race and class lines.

The most successful of these efforts was one between a very large and successful suburban church, 91st Street Christian Church, led by a wonderful pastor, Russ Blowers, and a remarkable young assistant minister, Tim Streett. As a young man, Tim had witnessed his father's (who was also a pastor) murder in a horrible, needless one-dollar robbery at his home. Tim subsequently dedicated his life to healing, rather than bitterness, and led his church into partnerships with urban groups. He built a partnership between his suburban church and Oasis of Hope, an urban church led by Reverend Frank Alexander, who is highly committed to revitalizing his neighborhood. The partnership has blossomed into a consortium of churches and has resulted in Jireh Sports, an inner-city sports ministry that builds the physical, moral, and spiritual muscle of many youths in the area.

Tim incisively remarks,

> Race is a huge initial barrier, as is neighborhood dynamics—a different culture, a different way things are done. Once you get over those barriers, there are still the cultural issues, and hopefully you can deal with those without race being a problem. If you have a brother or sister in Christ who is different from you, skinwise and culturally, whom you can go to and say 'help me understand this,' then it is easier to get past all the barriers. I had people with whom I could do that, but finding those sorts of relationships takes a very intentional effort. When those relationships are established, and there is trust, the other barriers start to come down.

Nevertheless, once those barriers are overcome, success is not automatic. Streett notes that there still are many bad examples of suburban churches starting with good intentions but unable to sustain their effort. The relationship with an urban church must be a true partnership. "One of the things that I think is important to recognize," he says, "is that a lot of the urban churches have the knowledge and the skill and . . . need to lead the effort, which helps them develop respect in their community."

Suburban churches, even when they possess considerable resources, typically do not offer the kind of help that urban churches want. Urban churches need to know that their suburban partners are there to serve them and to be co-laborers with them—not to be benefactors who have little interest in the long haul.

It is important to point out that resistance on the part of suburban churches is not necessarily racial. Many suburban churches are more comfortable with financing overseas missionary work. They do not have urban contacts, do not want to be exploited, and are nervous about—and relatively unfamiliar with—urban problems. They are also often unwilling to take a supportive, rather than a lead, role. When a suburban-urban partnership works, as it did between 91st Christian church and Oasis of Hope, the results are indeed wonderful. I witnessed the fruits of the partnership one Sunday morning when the 91st Street

Congregation erupted in enthusiasm and joy after the Oasis of Hope choir sang for them and Pastor Streett gave his testimony. Their worlds were becoming one. This was bridging social capital in the making.

### The Moral/Spiritual Approach

Steve Bonds is an entrepreneurial pastor of Campbell Chapel. The church is 100 years old, founded by Steve's great-grandfather. In 1990 they moved into the tough Haughville area, next to what was then a crime-ridden housing project. No one in the church wanted to make the move, but Steve thought it was the right thing to do because of the opportunity to minister in the area.

With the size of the building and the strategic location, the congregation began to discuss ways to reach out to the community and, because of its financial condition, the church needed to apply for grants to start programs. He raised some money from a wealthy Episcopal church and applied to a quasi-government group for scholarships to start a summer camp. Then Pastor Bonds faced his first true government dilemma: whether to join hands with the Indianapolis Housing Authority. The authority had received a $30 million grant from the federal Hope VI program, which funds the demolition and rebuilding of worn-out public housing. The housing authority was looking for partners to help prepare families for homeownership. The authority did not want to put people into the homes who would just face the same problems as before—no job skills, no education, no one to look after kids— and encouraged Bonds to apply for a $100,000 grant for GED training and after-school programs. He accepted the challenge and staked out his role as a provider of government-funded services.

From a community standpoint, people in the area knew that if they wanted a GED or computer training, or an after-school program, they should go over to Campbell Chapel. However, Bonds states, "I don't want to be known only as an agency. I want people to say, 'you want to hear some good singing on Sunday morning, go over to Campbell Chapel. You want to know the Bible, go to their Bible study.' We are a church, we want to be known for those types of things first." That said, like many faith-based leaders who have partnered with government, Bonds shows remarkable sophistication about the need to separate publicly funded programs from the church's other ministries. And, like many other faith-based leaders, he sees that publicly funded services complement ministry and add credibility. He says,

> The kids, they don't think of us as a church. They know
> us as the place that brought them bowling, brought

them to the beach. . . . They know us for the food, the
hamburgers, the skating. That's what's important to a
twelve-year-old kid. The greater community, they know
us as a church, but they also know us as helping people
for physical, educational, and social needs, and not so
much for spiritual ones. That's because we keep functions separate. When the students come in here, they
come in through the basement door; they don't even see
the sanctuary. We don't say, "before you start class
today you need to learn some Bible verses," we don't get
into all that. They come here to get their GED, and that
is what we focus on. . . . We don't say that they can't be
in the program unless they participate in some spiritual activity. We don't even bring it up. We keep it totally
separate. Sometimes a student may slip in the class-
room and let out a four-letter word and I will say, "hey,
watch it, you're in the house of the Lord." Because they
forget where they are. We don't try to convert people in
our program, but we do invite them to come to church
if they want to, and some of them come.

Bonds's efforts have helped dozen of people who have failed in other
more traditional placements and helped them succeed. He has placed
over ninety individuals in employment over the last three years and met
his contractual objectives. He is clear-eyed about the separation
between the public service he is offering and the rest of the spiritual
activities of the church, but in his mind he never separates the work he
is doing from the need in society for moral and spiritual rehabilitation.
And he believes that the renewed interest in faith-based solutions is an
outworking of this belief that many people share.

He simplifies his success as follows: "With the moral decline in our
culture, people are looking for something: they are looking for answers.
If you about to be hit by a Mack truck, your immediate reaction is 'Oh
God.' And that's what people are ready to say, 'Oh God, help me!' Let's
go back to the church; it's the last resort."

The need for a response grounded in faith also causes parents and
friends of those in trouble to look for a faith-based solution. Pastor
Bonds remembers a meeting with the Juvenile Court Judge Payne. The
judge said, "We have got a problem. Our psychologists, our social workers, our probation officers, are not getting through. I am seeing the
same kids come through. They are not listening to the warnings, the
counseling, and the therapy." Bonds recalls that Judge Payne suggested
that people of faith could get through to the young people. He started a

faith-based counseling program of which Bonds's church is a part. "If a kid gets in trouble and his Mom brings him to his probation officer, the officer can say, 'you've got a choice: you can talk to a social worker or myself, or we have got a list of churches which will provide spiritual counsel. They won't make you come to church, but they can talk about values with your son.' Some parents have said, 'I want that, because the other stuff isn't working.'"

Faith-based organizations can produce publicly important results simply because they are sincere and determined in their motivation, which itself serves a higher purpose. As Olgen Williams claims, "Ultimately, faith-based groups have more resources—which grow out of their belief in the power of God to effectively change lives—than social services groups. Christian groups can lead with faith without proselytizing, and they still get good results."

Faith also plays an enormous role in the commitment of the volunteers congregations have at their disposal. Tim Streett notes that what distinguishes enduring programs is the presence of a person who says, "I want to do this."

> They have a specific call from God to do some sort of ministry. You are going to find good people who are very committed—but I think you are going to find a whole lot less of them—in secular organizations. There you may find someone who has said, "I want to do this," so they go and get a Masters of Social Work and a job, and from 9-5 they work really hard to improve the life of a community. The difference is, are they going to have the passion to do this job when it gets really tough? When the job goes, when the funding goes, are they still going to be there? The answer is yes if they are called by God to do that kind of work. What we have at Jireh Sports are people who we have identified as being called to this specific work. And what we have done is said, "we will facilitate you, your vision and your passion, by providing funds, a place, and administrative help—you go do what you want to do, which is to love and serve kids."

A sacred place can also have a positive effect. Isaac Randolph, who helped guide the Front Porch Alliance and is now the executive director of Indianapolis's Ten Point Coalition, describes this well:

> Let me give you an example from our job training program. It's in a church because it's more convenient, but

we also push our programs into the church to make sure the pastor is there, a visible presence representing the congregation. I watched some young men who are part of our program—and most of whom have been incarcerated—come in, and they all had the usual gangster want-to-be look. But they walk in and there is a transformation that occurs. There are certain assumptions and expectations when you go into a church: there are expectations of peace and safety. There are certain assumptions that you are going to be told the truth, even if it hurts you. So that if a program which is generally of a secular nature is being conducted in a church, it provides an added safety net—both physical and spiritual. I am not just a number; our instructor cares about me. Why? Because she's a part of this church. The pastor comes in and they immediately straighten up. And the fact is that no matter how far from civil society we think these kids are, most of them have a thin thread to the church. Many were raised in the black church, usually by their grandmothers. Even though they have strayed now, there is still that fine thread, and that's why the preachers have the power they do. There is still an expectation that the church is not going to hurt me, that they value me. You go to a lot of secular organizations and they treat you like a number, they call your number. Literally, you are number 5, you're number 6. What's your social security number? We ask some of those kinds of questions, but they know we have a different philosophy. When they come in here, there is a lot that is assumed: "thou shalt not steal, thou shalt not lie." There are a whole bunch of dynamics, when combined, that make faith-based initiatives so powerful.

And, finally, religious organizations can bring a sense of hope to those who "are considered the least, the last, and the left out." Randolph expresses this in the following way.

The last thing you want in a civil society is people with no hope, because they have nothing to lose. When you talk about empowerment, that means bringing people together around a just and honorable cause. You have to recognize and use a prophetic voice, recognize injustice, and be able to speak and not be afraid of any repercussions. Why? Because you have the highest of moral grounds. Once you have stabilized an individual and you move that person to action, then you have the abili-

ty to transform that individual. This is the truest sense of empowerment, because it is truly people of faith reaching inside that person and
developing the power of the inner self.

Religious purposes and interests are well-suited for partnership
when they are aligned with an important secular interest. We enlisted
religious organizations in the effort to reduce teen pregnancy. The
campaign was important to government because teen births are statis-
tically more likely to end in harmful consequences to the mother and
the child. It was important to members of the faith community,
because they believe that children should be born to a married couple
and that men and women should honor their bodies and their future
marriages. Abstinence classes, peer programs and public health efforts
were complemented by sermons and other initiatives from within the
faith community.

Similarly, with regard to the value of work, I was pleased when our
archbishop pointed me to an Encyclical by Pope John Paul II on the
meaning and value of work. In *Laborem Exercens*, the Pope wrote in
1981 that work, despite how difficult it may be at times, "is something
that corresponds to man's dignity, that expresses this dignity and
increases it." He continues to write, "Work is a good thing for man—a
good for his humanity—because through work man not only transforms
nature, adapting it to his own needs, but he also achieves fulfillment as
a human being and indeed, in a sense, becomes 'more a human being.'"[4]

I was encouraged that the view of the church, based on religious
and moral values, underscored our public mission to move toward a
work-based welfare system. We had a public obligation to help people
provide for themselves and their children, to make the nobler goal of
family independence a legitimate public policy goal rather than the
degrading dependency of the old welfare system. The Church, to be
sure, serves people out of an even nobler and higher aim. Nonetheless,
from a public official's standpoint, it serves a vital public interest in a
way that can only be ignored to the detriment of the entire community.

It also serves communities well through its commitment to education. As mayor I was honored to serve as cochair of the Archdiocese
inner-city school fundraising drive. Indianapolis archbishop Daniel
Buechlein, in the face of enormous financial challenges, and instead of
backing away from the center-city children, made them a priority. He
was determined to present more children with a high quality education
in their neighborhood—and one with strong values. The archdiocese
school campaign, which turned out to be the most successful one in the
country, helped stabilize neighborhoods by giving parents options. The
effort raised capital money for the schools and tuition money for the
children. Middle-class parents often moved in order to exercise their

choice of schools. Additionally, the schools nicely mixed all the elements of community renewal: faith, values such as self-discipline and respect, hope for the future through skill development, and a strong stabilizing physical presence.

### The Accountability Approach

Closely related to the moral/spiritual approach is one that emphasizes the self-respect that comes from responsibility. This distinction can lead to very sharp differences in service provision from secular providers. Jay Height of the Nazarene Church's Shepherd Community Center on Indianapolis's tough near-east side strongly believes that compassion requires his organization to uphold high standards of accountability for the people they serve and to require them to work and provide for their families.

This conclusion was not a form of mean-hearted conservatism but rather derived from Jay's faith. He explains, "we are compelled to do what the Bible tells us to do and that is what drives us in our Christian compassion—to meet the needs. Yet it also challenges us to not be empowering folks to make wrong decisions. There is a sense of accountability that we have on account of our faith convictions." But he also combined this accountability with an uplifting message, usually grounded in faith. He continues:

> When folks come here for food or clothing we are going to share with them and uplifting message, something to encourage them, and offer to pray with them if they have needs. There is no forced religion, but if someone comes to us they are going to know we are Christians by our love. . . . I am not going to allow someone to live a destructive lifestyle and support them in doing so. If someone comes to us drunk and they want food, we tell them to go and sober up and come back and then we will talk. That's where the tough love comes in. It's unconditional love, but conditional outreach. I think you are going to see that attitude more prevalent among faith-based groups. . . . While I may love you as a drug addict or an alcoholic I'm not going to support that lifestyle. I need to help you get the tools to overcome your addictions.

One day, while I was visiting Jay at his community center, he led me to the back door, threw it open, and happily proclaimed that a homeless shelter adjacent to his center had closed. The shelter viewed itself as just that: a shelter. Repairing the individual, giving him or her confidence, forcing people to deal with underlying problems, and encouraging them to work were not even on the organization's radar screen. So, a person visiting Jay's center, who might want food and a bed without responsibility, could just walk next door. The organization was, in Jay's mind, undermining the success he was cultivating in the lives of people he was trying to serve.

Linda Kosh of the very active Metro Church in Indianapolis adds that too many faith-based organizations place too much of an emphasis on the spiritual aspects of someone's life, forgetting that people have other very important needs. In order to help rehabilitate a broken life, faith groups need to focus on a variety of needs, because the first step to accountable living may very well come from getting the mundane, the "nonspiritual," aspects of someone's life under control. She believes that a holistic ministry includes spiritual, mental, physical, financial, social, and even marital components. She says,

> We used to have a clothing pantry, and I know a lot of churches do that. It helps your conscience because you are doing something for others, but then you start seeing the same people over and over again. How can you say you are helping people when what you are really doing is aiding and continuing the situation to keep them along the same route, or letting them get worse? We decided to just try to help five or ten families . . . and to try to figure out what it is that keeps bringing them back to our door. Is it that they don't have a job, or child care or education? We stopped having a food and clothing pantry.

Taking a holistic approach to helping others necessarily involves an organization in financial, family, physical, personal, and spiritual problems. For faith-based organizations, holistic service requires calling people to live and perform at a higher level in every area of their lives. Frank Alexander, whose church runs a community development corporation and has citywide respect for its contribution to the well-being of its neighborhood, believes the perspective of faith-based organizations on holistic service is what sets them apart from their secular counterparts. He puts it this way:

> The motivation of many community development corporations, for instance, is to help people from a economic and social standpoint. My work always comes

from a motivation to help people become who God created them to be. So it's a spiritual motivation, and to
that end we are going to share a value system that is
not shared by a regular community development corporation. . . . The holistic idea carries with it an idea of
caring about people spiritually, economically, socially,
emotionally, what have you. The first thing we shared
with the people in apartments that we manage was to
let them know that we weren't just going to be landlords. We say, "We don't believe that God intended y'all
to be dependent, and we are coming in to help you
become more independent." And as new people come
into our programs, there is a covenant in the application materials so they understand that this is our goal.

What has long struck me as impressive and compelling about faith-
based organizations is their ability to balance profound compassion with
tough standards. The most effective congregations and faith-based organizations can expect high standards because they do their part to provide
a caring community. It is as if they are saying to the people they serve: we
will do our part to provide you with a community that can help you with
a range of needs, and in return, you need to learn to be a participating
member of the community, which is going to require that you change
some things. They generally want public programs that can help people
with basic human needs, but they uniformly understand that they, not
public agencies, can provide the real help people need to become independent, self-respectful, and participating members of a community.

For example, one of Indianapolis's leading African-American pastors, T. Garrott Benjamin, has boldly created a number of church-run
programs to help tackle head-on the problems that keep urban youth
from succeeding. He created the Respect Academy in the early 1990s to
instill self-respect and discipline among youth in the city. He has always
required enrollees to conduct themselves in an upright manner in a setting that looks as much like a military academy as it does a church. He
also created Boys to Men, a program based on a popular book he has
written, that works with the juvenile justice system and area high
schools to mentor boys with the goal of making them successful men.
The program requires parental involvement and celebrates the passage
of the boys into manhood. Pastor Benjamin's tough love is based in the
belief that adherence to clear rules helps prepare these young men for
more opportunity in the outside world. Pastor Benjamin is an urban
hero, the kind of reformer who understands that when people are supported and loved while held to high standards, they will achieve.

# Public Responsibility for Faith-Based Partnerships

None of the foregoing is meant to suggest that secular providers are without effect, but rather to point to the unique contribution faith-based organizations make to community solutions. There are, of course, unsuccessful programs of all kinds and stripes, religious and secular. For this reason, it is absolutely important that public managers understand the very real challenges of dealing with community-based and faith-based organizations.

Over the past fifteen years, I have learned that public preparedness for working with community change agents such as religious groups depends on three general things. First, public managers need to be clear about how they are going to demand and account for results. Second, they need to find the right kind of balance between public and religious efforts to improve the community. And third, they need to wisely choose the ways that they will help and support religious organizations, since not all forms of help are beneficial to the community as a whole.

## *Contracting for Results: Accountability and Measurement*

As mayor I wanted results. I wanted to work with the programs that were the most effective for the dollars spent. When you take this perspective, encouraging faith-based organizations to do more with city, state, and federal resources seems like one way to drive results. Correspondingly, the best faith-based service providers do not shy away from accountability and, in fact, believe that if results are the criteria by which programs are judged, they will become the providers of choice over time. They are confident that they produce what public managers want, if only they be given a reasonable chance to prove themselves. Research indicates that well-managed programs get results, even if research is limited and relatively new when it comes to the effectiveness of local faith-based organizations.

Public managers, of course, cannot wait for research before they begin to define results for their community. What is important for now is that they commit to working with results-focused organizations. They know that they need organizations that help keep youth out of the justice system and in school, that help people find jobs and stay employed, and that help people overcome a range of barriers that keep them in at-risk environments.

That being said, government needs to be careful in how it measures results, defines performance and reduces its regulations of methods and inputs. Determining what government should regulate and measure is always a challenge.

Regulatory burdens constantly plague efforts to work with effective organizations. These burdens come in many forms, beginning with credentialing. Well-intentioned state and federal bureaucrats insist on licensed professionals in many places from social workers to drug therapists. The standards have a purpose, of course, but they regulate inputs in a manner that often discriminates against faith-based providers.

This was the core of the now-famous Teen Challenge fight in Texas in which then-Governor George W. Bush intervened to allow Teen Challenge to receive funding despite the absence of required credentials. The average small faith-based group might produce the best results but cannot afford the premium for licensed drug therapists, masters in social work, or whatever. If required credentials are not necessary for producing a desired result, then they should be dispensed with.

Sometimes public accountability translates into unworkable building codes. While I was with several pastors from across the country at the announcement of the White House Office of Faith-Based and Community Initiatives, they began expressing a concern that I often heard as mayor: "We can't afford to participate in certain public programs because the building costs are so high due to building code rules that have nothing to do with safety."

Many community organizations simply can not afford required retrofits to their buildings, expensive equipment installation, and minute requirements relating to configuration of space. In his book, *The Death of Common Sense*, Philip Howard documents how Mother Teresa's order of sisters were prevented from converting two New York City buildings into a homeless shelter.[5] The sisters spent a year gathering necessary permits only to have their plans dashed by a requirement that they install an elevator in their four-story building, though it was evident that they would not need an elevator. City codes in this case got in the way of a service that would have surely yielded results that would have benefited the city's public mission. Yet, it is often not clear to bureaucrats writing codes where safety ends and silliness begins.

In terms of outputs or outcomes, public agencies and publicly funded programs are frequently unclear about what they should be counting as success. Government regulators often measure activities: how many cases have been handled, how many people showed up for a training class, how many people successfully completed the program, and so it goes. Faith groups typically look for something more than this. They are more interested in whether or not the graduate of their programs has the strength and self-confidence to succeed on his or her own.

This definition of success is the reason Jay Height wants those in his shelter to pray and work and why Frank Alexander wants to be not merely a landlord but someone who encourages people to reach independence. Tim Streett knows he is being successful by the number of youth at Jireh Sports who begin to do the kinds of things that exceed the usual expectations of their peers. He describes with pride how Jireh's director helped one boy learn how to dive, coached and mentored him, and then watched in amazement as the boy won the city championship only one year after taking up the sport. The boy now trains with top divers at the Indiana-Purdue University Natatorium downtown Indianapolis. Other youth at Jireh, who read at grade levels below their own, begin to catch up and then succeed academically because they discover the joy of learning.

These kinds of successes, Tim surmises, are based on a very clear idea of what counts as a legitimate outcome. No one would even dream of measuring success by counting the number of programs offered in a year or the number of youth served. It is what happens with those youth that counts and should be counted.

Olgen Williams, engrained in both faith and community efforts, discusses the issue of results this way:

> Faith groups have a higher standard of success, but not necessarily as tangible as regular secular efforts. We can't take away the value of people. Faith values people for who they are, not as a number, not a product. They feel different when they know they are not just a number. We see results in changed lives. Sometimes we just sow a seed and may not realize the results for years. But we do see people change; we've got some great stories. More tangible documentation of success comes from things like reduction of crime, which can't be attributed only to secular services. But it is hard to always show which program has helped. We had a group that worked with abused children, and they wanted to trace how their program had affected the neighborhood. But it was too hard because a combination of programs often make the change, they all contribute to the process. . . . That's why you need to support a variety of programs. I document success by living in my neighborhood. Who's still hanging out on the corner, who's not. I listen, I can see the difference. I may not keep a strict record of how many gunshots I hear a day, but I know if they are decreasing.

Clearly, the creation of a results culture requires that outcomes be defined by how well people are doing rather than how many of them are being served. Once that is understood and put into practice, however, there needs to be a recognition of other forms of public goods that are not as easy to define.

Early in my first mayoral term, I put out a Request for Proposals for a program that would use dollars traditionally reserved for community centers. I made clear that community service providers would now be measured on how many of their citizens secured and kept jobs. The centers and their advocates erupted angrily, claiming that their presence in the community, as safe places for seniors to gather and for citizens to gain valuable information, provides an indispensable social good. Balancing these somewhat conflicting domains of performance—individual or neighborhood, social capital in general or actual jobs in particular—remained a constant struggle during my years as mayor.

What matters the most from a public management perspective is consistency and fairness over the long haul. Over time, a steady emphasis on results will make a positive difference. This helps prevent the perception that public officials are reaching out to the faith community merely because they secretly want to impose their religious beliefs on others through their public jobs or because they favor religious groups as a way to shake up public agencies that they do not like. We continually emphasized that results were our guiding light, and that we were reaching out to faith groups because we thought they could generate the right kinds of outcomes. One community leader says, "Goldsmith's argument was, 'Find those who are most effective, and if they are running an effective after-school program—I don't care if they are green-eyed Martians—we should help them.'"

Performance measurement in social services will remain a difficult endeavor. Input measures are the norm, and some of them are even appropriate. And certainly, faith-based organizations need to be held accountable for the dollars they spend and the processes they manage. But the public management of the future, if it is to be true to its role as the custodian of the citizens' resources, must recognize that it has an obligation to open up service provision to *all* potential candidates. The government contract officer of the future, in an effort to truly focus on results, needs to invest in educating faith-based organizations and other nontraditional providers about the ins and outs of public services.

This will pay off over time as competition is enhanced by a larger, more diverse, pool of viable providers. The public managers of the future will also turn a sharper eye to licensing and code enforcement, making sure that the public good is not sacrificed to marginally important (or worse, meaningless) regulations that give everyone headaches and help no one. Aggressiveness on this front is the difference between acceptable returns on public investments and wasteful, mediocre performance. It is also the key to cultivating an environment where success becomes the standard.

### The Right Balance

Like the "compassionate conservatism" that President Bush espouses, we rejected the extremes in our efforts in Indianapolis: we rejected the notion that faith-based organizations should pick up the social welfare responsibility of government, and we rejected the view that government should be the monopolist of neighborhood good deeds, namely that all its assistance should be delivered through a government-like bureaucracy. It is disingenuous to believe one sector can operate by ignoring the other. As Rebecca Blank notes in *It Takes a Nation*, all religious congregations in America would have to raise hundreds of thousands of additional dollars annually to replace just a few federal programs on which the elderly poor depend.[6]

This is a reality that cannot be ignored. We also cannot ignore the inexcusable wastefulness of federal programs that have often funded mediocrity while high-performing faith groups are running on a shoestring. What we wanted to do in Indianapolis is build up the capacity and reach of faith solutions so that they could perform as competent partners but remain the heralded small platoons of compassion.

We discovered that government needed to exercise great care in working with its faith partners, and the partners needed to exercise even more care in working with us. There is a kind of balancing act that occurs between government and religious organizations that, when successful, maximizes what is best about each. We learned that many of the stereotypes of faith-based organizations are simply wrong or highly exaggerated, especially when government is committed to outreach and education. Whatever else may have been achieved by our outreach to faith and community groups, we were most often complimented for countering the conventional governmental attitude that faith-based organizations are inherently poorly run, that they are not effective in changing lives, and that they should basically be ignored by public managers.

For instance, most faith-based organizations that partnered with city hall were not out to get government money without accountability, were not ignorant about the key issues involved, and were not about to let themselves be secularized by public funds. We learned that those on the left, who fear that religious organizations will constantly be infringing on the religious freedoms of their clients, were caricaturing these groups, and that those on the right who feared that these groups would simply be secularized and "taken over" by government did not give them enough credit for their ability to protect their mission.

Instead of living up to the caricatures, the faith-based organizations with whom we partnered were marked by a solid understanding of the key issues involved. In particular, they understood what was permissible with government funds, they recognized that partnerships in which they participated served a public benefit, and they were willing to subject themselves to government audits and checks.

*Clear-eyed distinctions between what is and is not permissible with government funds.* Steve Bonds operates a faith-based organization whose spiritual mission is very important, but his understanding of what he does as a state contractor is just as clear. He makes it known to anyone with whom he discusses the church's role over against the state that under no circumstances will they ask a client to participate in other church activities. His simple rule of thumb is, "We don't even bring it up. We keep it totally separate."

Isaac Randolph says that "it's not necessary for an urban church to proselytize" because its mission can be partially fulfilled "by just being there and doing the work." Faith-based organizations in cities deal with a range of problems. They can address material needs with public funds and spiritual needs with private funds, but any type of service can further the mission of the church even while it is furthering the purposes of government. Urban congregations have a de facto moral authority, and using public funds in strict accordance with the regulations that govern them does not diminish that authority. There is a moral effect on program clients simply because of what the congregation stands for and does in the community, and this effect is felt even in the absence of direct proselytization or worship, Randolph says.

On the flip side, Jay Height says that he will generally stay away from government money because he does not like to have to compartmentalize his programming. He says, "We don't get government commodities for our food pantry, because they told us we couldn't pray with folks. That's fine." What is important, he adds, is that he has the right relationship with government. He needs to know that he can call someone in government for help, whether it concerns getting an alley closed or getting the police to show up for community meetings. Just as there are government funds that do not fit his ministry, there are also private funds that are inappropriate. What matters is that the right kind of relationship is in place, because only then "do you get the trust level and the give-and-take necessary to know how to best work with and support each other."

Height's comments demonstrate an understanding of partnerships that involve financial resources. He and others who are more receptive to receiving public funds understand that government's purposes dictate that its funds be used in a certain way. And, like the others, he respects that. In general, most active faith-based organizations that I have encountered know very well what the limits of public resources are, how they may be used, and whether or not it is a good idea for their organization to receive them.

*Understanding that services, first and foremost, serve a public purpose and have a public benefit.* A good partnership starts with each party clearly understanding what the other needs. The better faith-based groups in Indianapolis understood their role in producing a public good or benefit. They knew that public agencies were interested in them as partners who could help get people jobs, reduce crime, provide care for children, and so on. And so long as the goals of their public agency partners were congruent with their goals, they did not feel exploited, but rather were pleased to be a complementary partner.

Rev. Alexander remembers a time when he directed a Christian community center and began receiving public funds for training programs he had designed. He ran the first day-care teacher training course in the state and expanded to include job training. His board of directors, he recalls, "said that we didn't have any business taking government money. But my question was how are we going to empower people so they can make a living? 'If you are telling me that we can't accept resources that serve a purpose like this,' I said, 'then I'm leaving.' And I left." Rev. Alexander says that he was interested in combating the perception, which exists both within churches and in the media, that religious groups do not really care about producing publicly beneficial services, which explains why he adamantly opposed his board.

Partnerships with public agencies are a way to demonstrate that faith-based organizations truly do care about reducing crime, helping move people out of poverty, and providing good and safe learning environments for our children. Many religious organizations across the nation engage in such partnerships precisely because they care about improving their communities.

Some people harbor a view of faith-based organizations as clandestine evangelizers—people who say they will comply with government but only really care about pushing their faith on others. If this view were true, we would see more court cases on this issue. Despite evidence that the number of faith-based government contractors has increased since the passage of welfare reform, there have been very few—and almost no—lawsuits alleging First Amendment violations. Most faith-based organizations out there are doing good that we should recognize as just that—good.

*Openness to audits and performance demands.* When we first contracted with neighborhood churches to maintain their small inner-city parks, the city demanded accountability: The church could use volun-

teers and could build up its standing in the neighborhood as an important and contributing asset. The citizens could see the cleanliness
increase and the graffiti decrease. But if the church did not perform
daily as the city contract anticipated, then the contract needed to be
cancelled, no matter how valuable its Sunday service and other ministries might be. The basis of the contract was to create a safe, clean
place to play. We employed monitors who reported on the parks' condition, and sometimes our faith partners needed warnings. Our faith
partners accepted performance and financial accountability as a fair
and appropriate expectation.

In fact, some of our faith-based organizations actually appreciated
the accountability. Linda Kosh at Metro Church is clear about the fact
that making use of public resources adds a level of accountability to a
faith-based organization's operations that is not only necessary, but is
good. "I know a lot of people are after 'faith-based dollars,'" she says,
"but they don't want the accountability that comes with those dollars—
and I'm against that. You have to be responsible to whoever gives you
money. I would rather have [what comes with responsibility, such as
paperwork,] than someone putting the money where it is not supposed
to go or using it improperly."

Complying with accountability measures is sometimes equated
with becoming secularized, but performance standards do not need to
arouse this fear. In fact, this fear is overblown, says Olgen Williams. He
claims that the real problem with standards is that they too often
devolve into burdensome and unnecessary regulations. But they cannot be blamed for secularization. Even though government tends to go
overboard in stipulating what is allowable or not, which in turn results
in too much paperwork, he claims that the fear of secularization is
overblown. "If you compromise your program, you can't blame it on
the government," he plainly states. "Compromise only happens when
you are chasing dollars. If your motives are pure, government money
isn't going to hurt the program. To become secularized is really an
individual choice."

Faith-based organizations across the nation have been quick to
understand the realities of public accountability. I recall a moment during the media question-and-answer session following the announcement of the White House Office of Faith-Based and Community
Initiatives. One of the media representatives was questioning the
Reverend Mark Scott, who was associated with the remarkably successful Boston Ten Point Coalition. The Coalition had greatly helped
Boston cut its juvenile homicide rate by more than 90 percent through
the street-level activism of concerned pastors. But the reporter wanted
to know about financial accountability. Reverend Scott simply respond-

ed, "we will account for all funds and simply open our books if you wish"—a response that diffused suspicion. His confidence in their bookkeeping and willingness to disclose any and all information is commendable and becoming more common among religious groups as they understand the nature of public partnerships.

The 2001 release of the White House report, "Unlevel Playing Field," which documents the wide federal neglect of faith-based organizations as potential service providers, revealed that nonprofit government contractors often have not been held to performance standards. The entrance of faith-based organizations into the picture has suddenly generated an interest in performance standards in human services, but it would be unfair to hold them to standards that are not being applied to other organizations. Instead, because of their understanding of accountability, faith-based organizations are in a good position to help redefine the issue of successful performance at the community level.

### Ways of Helping

Government can assist faith organizations in a number of ways. Government and the recipient agency each have choices for how they frame their partnership. At its simplest level government can stop funding policies that run counter to the values that it and the rest of America consider important. Ending Aid to Families with Dependent Children, the old welfare system, and the financial incentives it provided to mothers to have children outside of marriage is an example of this. But there exist other ways that government can improve partnerships with faith-based organizations without large legislative changes. Three in particular warrant mention.

#### Even and Friendly Playing Field

In the words of Isaac Randolph, the Front Porch Alliance set out to facilitate faith-based interventions simply by convening stakeholders. He aptly describes our outreach model this way:

> By convening people, government can bring together those who would not or could not come together on their own. If the mayor calls, people will show up, whether they like him or not, sometimes they just show up to see who else will be there. If preacher A calls a meeting, Preacher B may not come.

When government acts as a convener, it reaches out to all potential partners and stakeholders. We worked hard to make sure that we did not take the conventional approach to solving problems, namely over-funding existing government delivery systems. By convening the right players, problems can often be solved more creatively, at less cost, and with better results.

For example, Jay Height's faith-based community center wanted to expand their facilities but could not get past the real estate division of the local electric company. During a tour, the staff described to me the promising things they could do if they could secure the relatively deso-late piece of land, which was an old, nonfunctioning station of the elec-tric company. Height explains the circumstances this way:

> Why I believe the Front Porch Alliance was so critical, so positive, has absolutely nothing to do with money. And that's what I believe has gotten lost in the nation-al debate. The money that we got was very little; some people think Goldsmith gave us tons of money, but he didn't. For example, Goldsmith called the CEO of Indianapolis Power and Light, and they had a closed substation right behind our property. And the mayor said, "Why don't you give the property to them." And [the CEO] said, "Sure." Then his attorneys had seizures and said, "You can't do that, we're a public company," and so on. And so what they did was give us a cash donation that was close to the purchase price, and we were able to buy it. It was that ability to have someone say, "This is a group who is doing good work, you should work with them." The legacy which I believe the Front Porch Alliance and the Mayor left with the city, is that he said, "Faith-based groups are OK."

In this case, the electric company and the homeless shelter simply needed to be matched up. They needed someone to convene their inter-ests. The shelter also needed someone to introduce them to an estab-lished community entity as a viable solution to a problem—albeit an unconventional solution.

City leaders can also create an even and friendly playing field by clearing away obstacles and solving problems that might otherwise overwhelm a small faith-based organization. Like the peace garden that I described in Chapter One, which required fifty-three separate approvals, land issues often require lots of obstacle removal. Jireh Sports has had a bit of experience with working through the challenges of getting a ministry in the right kind of property. Streett explains the kind of assistance that helps in instances such as these:

> The Front Porch Alliance's job was to remove obstacles. . . . We are a small group which can do good things, but we don't know how to jump through bureaucratic hoops, necessarily. But more than anything, here is the key, if it were just up to our program staff at Jireh, we would never get through those hoops. . . . I don't know how some small grassroots groups survive [without help navigating city bureaucracy]. In our case it wasn't so much fiscal things [which FPA assisted with] but things like someone who helped us walk through the rezoning process for a warehouse we acquired.

*Financial Resources*

Another important role that government plays, says Isaac Randolph, is to leverage funds—which goes beyond simply giving out funds. He says,

> Government is good at putting proper resources on the table. And that sends a couple of messages. One, there is this feeling government always backs a winner. So we had the ability to spread out the risks that are associated with backing very small projects. The Front Porch Alliance leveraged dollars, so that when we put a dollar on the table, three other dollars usually quickly followed—either by virtue of showing people how to secure additional contributions or acting as sort of a stamp of approval for foundations and other donors.

Government can help with money in a variety of ways. The Indianapolis effort did not involve much local money. Some of the funding came from tax abatement fees that we charged businesses. The competitive awards of $5,000-$10,000 that we created out of these fees were designed more to celebrate an important neighborhood effort and to give it a bit of help than to be a comprehensive source of funding. Clearly, the money we gave groups constituted a very small amount of the organizations' funding.

One advantage of small funding amounts is that they encourage other sources of funding and prevent government from being too dominant an influence or source of pressure. We found it important to draw attention to the grants so that other funding sources would step up to the plate. In this case, we handed out the financial awards on a quarterly basis in a public ceremony that recognized a neighborhood garden, or a new playground or some other tangible accomplishment of a community group. The celebratory nature of the event invariably attracted the interest of others in the community. Every community has people that want to bet on a winner, and thus it is important to showcase the winners in a regular fashion.

Other forms of government participation also seem broadly acceptable. Few would quarrel that the government can use its tax policy to encourage charitable giving. It obviously is more efficient for me to contribute directly to my synagogue and have it help those left behind, than for government to tax me and then run a process that grants the dollars back to the synagogue. This is the logic involved in the White House's effort in 2001 to encourage charitable giving by granting a credit to people who give, and especially those who do not itemize their tax returns.

On a continuum from least to most controversial, the next best way for a faith-based organization to benefit from government money occurs when the benefits follow the recipient—that is, in the form of a voucher. A voucher for child care allows the parent to pick from a variety of providers. As a total percentage, faith-based organizations deliver a lot of child care. The advantage to a voucher, other than the choice it gives the parent, is simply that government is little involved in the operations of the provider.

The issue that generates the most heated debate centers on the direct provision of public money to the faith provider. No one really argues that public money should be used for specifically religious purposes, but should it be used by a religious organization to carry out a public responsibility such as providing shelter to the homeless or job training to former welfare recipients? I have always taken the position that religious organizations should also have the right to apply for government money like anyone else. Thus, the Front Porch Alliance helped groups apply for government grants.

"If there is something city hall can help me with," one community leader said of our work, "it is telling me, who I can call—someone who can say, 'in HUD this money is available, this is money you can go after, here's how you do it, here's how you apply for it.'" A Catholic-schools program received abstinence education dollars with the help from the Front Porch Alliance. The Alliance acted as an advocate, explaining to state officials why they should not discriminate against a faith-based provider. Some of the evangelical church leaders who generally supported my efforts as mayor preferred not to participate in any program with government dollars, which was fine. However, this principled position should be available to a religious organization as a choice, not imposed on it by a bureaucrat administering a biased system.

Similarly, some of the advocates for a very high wall between church and state believe that no money should go to faith organizations. This position argues essentially that any organization, except those that are religious, should be able to compete for the money that pays for food and shelter or a similar public good. I have never been able to see this view as anything other than discriminatory.

The possibility of government money altering the mission of the faith group certainly exists, but as Olgen Williams points out, the church, mosque, or synagogue should be able to decide whether applying for the funds is worth the risk. The idea that religious groups should not receive government money for fear of being corrupted essentially legitimizes the discrimination, suggesting that these organizations do not know what is in their best interest and do not have the wherewithal to say no.

Government money, no doubt, carries risks. On a day-to-day basis, though, these risks have less to do with secularizing forces than with the strain they place on the practical operations of small organizations. The risks that come with government funding are the same for all community-based organizations, not just faith-based groups. The human capital and administrative infrastructure required to comply with many government stipulations is a form of discrimination in itself: government favors large organizations for no reason other than its inability, or unwillingness, to simplify its requirements and do away with unnecessary regulations. Pastor Bonds puts a human face on this predicament for small organizations:

> The government is sometimes slow in processing our paperwork, and we have to wait longer than a month to get paid. We are still waiting on moneys that we submitted over six weeks ago, for example. Large nonprofit agencies that have the same contracts that we do are multimillion-dollar agencies. They can borrow from Peter to pay Paul, where we don't have that luxury. The type of staff I have, most of them work here from 9:00 to 3:00, part time, and many of them have to rely on other income. So if you are here to get rich, you are in the wrong place. You are going to get your money, but it isn't going to be in a timely fashion. That's why a lot of

churches don't want government grants. . . . A lot of
churches are saying, "How am I going to get someone to
work for thirty days before they get paid? I don't want
no part of that, all the paperwork, and if they don't like
my paperwork I won't get paid. Thanks, but no
thanks."

Of course, we cannot expect government contracting processes to
change overnight, and thus faith-based organizations must have their
eyes wide open when considering public funding. Government funding
can create a great opportunity for a faith-based provider to leverage the
money to attract additional funding, and it can stretch the organization's influence. But faith-based organizations should avoid participation when their goals and government's goals do not match.

Some organizations, especially those that are hard-pressed financially, may try to alter their mission to match the goals that the government lays out in contract application guidelines. I once gave a talk
in Augusta, Georgia, after which a pastor told a reporter that he would
give up his Bibles if necessary to get more resources into his neighborhood. One has to wonder if the trade-off would help in the long run.
While no pastor should ever have to sacrifice sacred texts for resources
in the first place, this pastor was showing very clearly that a tough
choice may be involved.

While the Charitable Choice clause in several federal programs
helps preserve the integrity of religious organizations, these groups
have to decide for themselves whether or not they are suited to the stated aims and stipulations of a government program. Once a contract is
signed, government officials forget all the anecdotes and good things
they heard about the contractor: from then on, they expect the organization to fulfill the terms of the contract.

*Authority*

Along with convening and leveraging resources, Isaac Randolph likes to
point out that government has the ability to shine a light on successful
programs. This has a way of attracting attention and resources to effective community builders, and it also helps shape the public debate about
the best ways to solve community problems. Isaac says,

Highlighting the work of successful groups is probably
one of the most underrated things that government can
accomplish. It means getting to know a program and
talking about them to the media, talking about them to

the community. Typically some of the best programs are the best because the people running them don't have time to blow their own horn. They are too busy making children into good citizens, feeding the hungry, teaching the illiterate, all those things, which take a lot of time and labor.

When it highlights success, government elevates standards and makes previously marginalized organizations visible to the public. It grants legitimacy to groups that do not have the ability or desire to market themselves. Tim Streett sums up his experience with the Front Porch Alliance this way:

> More than anything, what mattered most was just the attitude of the Mayor's office to recognize the legitimacy of our mission. And to be able to say to others, here is someone who is doing something legitimate. I would have to say that that was the most helpful thing about the Front Porch Alliance, more than anything tangible. I know this kind of help is intangible, but it's very important. And it takes place at no cost to the city, other than having someone who knew what was going on who could introduce us to others.

This form of intangible help does not really remain intangible for long. Once a community gets to know faith-based organizations and other grassroots groups as potential partners, they attract the attention of additional public agencies, foundations, and corporations. People and organizations that formerly would never consider joining up forces with them begin to call them up, invite them to meetings, and introduce them to their networks.

Not long after we helped launch the Indianapolis Ten Point Coalition, the pastors involved in the coalition began getting calls from other agencies and organizations. I remember a meeting that we had organized in my conference room to deal with a security issue that had arisen at our downtown mall during the weekends. Youth were becoming reckless after mall hours on the streets around the mall and had even begun damaging property. We invited the Ten Point Coalition's chairman, Reverend Charles Harrison, to the meeting to see if perhaps any of the pastors would be willing to help provide some monitoring on the streets.

A variety of law enforcement and justice system officials were present, and as they heard Reverend Harrison describe how he thought the pastors could help, they began bringing up other "opportunities" for the coalition. Would the pastors be willing to mentor probationers? Would they be willing to help out with juvenile offender mediations? Could they help get community policing implemented in $x$ neighborhood? And so on. One of my assistants smiled at Reverend Harrison and asked, "Are you still happy you guys have been so successful?" Reverend Harrison simply sighed. The Ten Point Coalition had quickly become a partner of choice in Indianapolis, and they began accessing funding sources traditionally unavailable to grassroots, community-based organizations.

Government can also use its authority to connect citizens to faith-based organizations. Judge James Payne began referring young offenders to a faith-based character education organization whose constituency was generally middle-class and suburban. He did so because he knew the program was solid, not because it had a tradition of serving urban juvenile offenders. Most people never would have thought that the program was well suited to serving Indianapolis youth who had run into trouble with the law. Judge Payne used his authority to make the organization a legitimate referral place for youth in need of help. The youth would never have chosen or known about the program otherwise.

The judge had presided over tens of thousands of delinquency and neglect cases, often noting with frustration the failures from traditional social service placements. In order to find more options for interventions he reached out to faith-based organizations diverse in both ethnicity and religion. If the faith option was appropriate and preferred by the parents, limited government funding would flow from the court to pay for the placement. These were additional options, and of course did not displace more traditional secular placements.

Authority, of course, is a tricky thing. Public officials must take care never to use their position to direct people to faith-based programs against their will. They also have to take care not to tip the playing field in the other direction by favoring only faith-based groups or by giving preference to just a few of their favorites when a contracting opportunity presents itself. There are always opportunities for government to abuse its authority, no matter what the issue is. The best safeguard against abuse is to have clearly stated objectives for a program and a transparent process for identifying and working with community partners.

Faith-based solutions certainly will not solve all our problems, but they need to be considered an option far more frequently and consistently than they are at present. We are at a point in history where we need to consider their contribution to society honestly and dispassionately. The recent public debate on this issue, at times, has grown divisive and too ideological. There are practical realities about faith solutions that are not at all divisive—in fact, they are unifying and healing in their impact. Working through these practical issues is now our first priority.

*Endnotes*

[1] *Giving USA*, AAFRC Trust for Philanthropy (2000).

[2] *Giving and Volunteering in the United States*, Independent Sector (1999).

[3] Robert Putnam, *Bowling Alone: The Collapse and Revival of American Community* (New York: Simon and Schuster, 2000), 22 ff.

[4] Pope John Paul II, *On Human Work (trans. of Laborum Exercens)* (Washington, D.C.: United States Catholic Conference), II, 9.

[5] Philip K. Howard, *The Death of Common Sense: How Law Is Suffocating America* (New York: Random House, 1994).

[6] Rebecca Blank, *It Takes a Nation: A New Agenda for Fighting Poverty* (Princeton: Princeton University Press, 1997).

CASE STUDY

# The Neighborhood Empowerment Initiative in Three Indianapolis Neighborhoods
## Practices as Principles

**Ryan Streeter**

Ryan Streeter is Director of the Resource Center at the Office of Faith-Based and Community Initiatives, U.S. Department of Housing and Urban Development. He authored the following case study while serving as a research fellow at Hudson Institute. Streeter has written, edited, and contributed to several books on the public importance of the institutions of civil society, including *Transforming Charity* (Hudson Institute, 2001) and *Religion and the Public Square in the 21st Century* (Hudson Institute, 2001).

In his inaugural mayoral address, delivered in January 1992, Indianapolis Mayor Stephen Goldsmith declared:

> The soul of our city is in its neighborhoods, and government needs to remake itself around those neighborhoods. We need to break up large government. We need to look at more efficient ways to deliver services. We need to help citizens take back their neighborhoods, take back their government, take back their own responsibilities.
>
> We need to find a way to empower the people and the private organizations that live in this city—to suggest that if they have a better way to provide services, if they know what is in their best interest more than government does, then let them provide those services through their own community organizations, through their own religious organizations, as partners with the city of Indianapolis.

Eight years later, his final "State of the City" address was titled "The State of Our Neighborhoods: Setting the Standard for Tomorrow." The speech celebrated a vastly improved city whose citizens had greater economic opportunity and were in greater control of their communities. Unemployment was steady at a little more than 2 percent, one of the lowest rates among American cities, and nearly 50,000 new jobs had been created. Neighborhood associations had boomed as residents got involved in neighborhood affairs. And the city had helped build 6,000 homes to help thousands of families realize the rewards of homeownership.

*Putting Faith in Neighborhoods* shines a light on the centrality of neighborhood revitalization to the Goldsmith administration's overall vision for Indianapolis. It was interwoven with almost every other major initiative the city undertook. And while the city received accolades and attention for its efficiency through competition and its economic vigor during the Goldsmith administration, very little has been learned outside Indianapolis from the city's empowerment efforts other than the Front Porch Alliance (FPA).[1] FPA was only a part—albeit a very important part—of a broader initiative to strengthen neighborhoods and encourage municipal citizenship.

This case study looks at three of the eight neighborhoods in which the Goldsmith administration invested time and resources to give greater control to neighborhood residents. Its purpose is to contribute to the revival of interest in community-based solutions to urban predicaments in order to help urban leaders, policymakers, and neighborhood entrepreneurs understand the promise and complexity of municipal citizenship.

Each of the three neighborhoods considered here is a unique community with a unique history. Each had a very different experience with the city's empowerment effort. And each saw different outcomes as a result of the strategy.

But the neighborhoods also have much in common. All of them had watched their general economic and social condition deteriorate since the 1960s. All three have seen businesses—and the jobs provided by the businesses, and the incomes provided by the jobs—depart for other communities. All experienced unacceptably high levels of crime. And they watched their civic infrastructure stagnate over time as residents lost hope in the future of their neighborhoods. It is difficult for citizens to change their neighborhoods when the neighborhoods do not seem worth changing.

As Goldsmith has pointed out, the Indianapolis approach to empowerment during his administration was based on the simple idea that residents need to be given more of a say in their communities and more real control over the governance decisions that affect them. While citizen participation must be handled in tandem with other efforts to renovate buildings and houses, repair the physical infrastructure, help small businesses, and fund human services agencies in the community, empowerment was never conceived in terms of these kinds of efforts alone. Without active citizens to take ownership of their neighborhoods, all these additional efforts would not produce the kind of change that would last over time.

Helping citizens to effectively participate in the life of their community does not produce change overnight. Citizen engagement involves the hearts, minds, and habits of people. Improvements as a result of their active participation can only be measured over a significant period of time. This case study therefore takes objective data into account in so far as they help paint a picture of the overall condition of the neighborhood and, where appropriate, help us understand the Goldsmith administration initiatives that were in some way directly related to them.

Interviews were conducted with leaders and residents in each neighborhood. Nearly one hundred people were consulted, but as in any community, there are core groups of leaders in each neighborhood to whom everyone else refers researchers such as my team and myself. These leaders are people who have been consistently involved in their neighborhoods over time and who had significant experience with the Goldsmith administration's empowerment initiatives. My colleagues and I conducted more extensive interviews with more than forty of these leaders, both over the phone, in one-on-one interviews, and in group discussions. They were asked to explain what they understood neighborhood empowerment to be, what kinds of changes they had seen in their communities during Goldsmith's administration, and what they thought of the effectiveness of the administration's neighborhood initiatives.

The interviews are more than a purely subjective account of whether or not people feel empowered. They reveal the nature of municipal citizenship in the neighborhood, namely the degree to which the residents have the capacity to design community projects, collaborate with city officials, and make effective decisions about the future of their community. There was an uncanny similarity in the results of interviews with people from the same neighborhood. Perhaps it is not so uncanny when one considers that each of these neighborhoods has a relatively distinctive identity, comprises a geographic area no larger than a small town, and has no more than 17,000 residents. And, while most low-income, urban neighborhoods have a subaverage number of businesses and community assets, many of their residents use the same grocery stores, go to the same churches, play in the same parks.

The most likely reason for the uniformity, however, is the umbrella-organization strategy that Goldsmith used to unify each neighborhood's efforts. Almost everyone we interviewed, from residents who held no official "neighborhood leader" status to police officers, had some experience coordinating their community activity with others through the umbrella organization. While there was substantive disagreement within the communities regarding strategies and priorities, the uniformity was much more remarkable. The nature of municipal citizenship is very much dependent on how people choose to coordinate their activity and what kinds of projects they undertake together.

## Empowerment in Three Neighborhoods:
## The Challenge of "Little Republics"

The United States has more than 3,000 counties and more than 16,000 townships. If individual states embody unique qualities and pose challenges to the implementation of federal policies within them, how much more distinct and challenging are these even smaller jurisdictions? All the more complex, then, is the character of multiple individual neighborhoods. Each is distinct, each its own small entity.

Though not usually recognized as independent governing authorities, many neighborhoods have the characteristics of active, little republics. Residents select, either directly or by their tacit consent, certain neighbors to represent their interests at local meetings, they fight over resources and where to implement them, and in the best-case scenario, they care about character and place a lot of responsibility for their neighborhood's well-being on themselves. Each of the three neighborhoods in this study has a distinct identity. The Goldsmith umbrella organization policy strengthened the identities and motivated significant expressions of self-governance.

The three neighborhoods that we studied are the near-west side, the southeast side, and Martindale-Brightwood. The near-west side is often referred to as "the WESCO area," after its umbrella organization, the West Side Cooperative Organization (WESCO). It is a racially mixed neighborhood of 10,300 residents. The southeast side, a predominantly white neighborhood of 16,500, is sometimes referred to as "the SUMO area," after its umbrella organization, the Southeast Umbrella Organization. Martindale-Brightwood is a mainly African-American neighborhood of 9,500.[2]

As I said earlier, each neighborhood faced considerable challenges when Goldsmith took office. The near-west side was arguably in the worst condition, but all three struggled with problems rooted in decades-long decay and manifested in drugs, joblessness, crime, and hurting families.

### The Near-West Side

Urban residents across Indianapolis have come to view the near-west side somewhat jealously. It is Indianapolis's "miracle story." It has overcome sizable odds to become an example of renewal through grassroots citizenship. Residents outside the neighborhood often attribute its success to the amount of funding it has received and the special attention it received from city officials and outside observers.

While some of the jealousy might be justified, it tends to obscure the fact that the WESCO neighborhood was in bad shape in the early 1990s. All the usual indicators of urban decay were alive and well on the near-west side. Its streets were practically a distribution center for Indianapolis's crack-cocaine epidemic, and when two arson investigators were shot in the neighborhood in the early 1990s, its criminals sent a signal to the authorities that they were in control. Its turnaround is nothing short of dramatic and has come through the investment of much collective energy and activity.

The neighborhood was originally a "melting pot" in the standard sense of that term. In the late nineteenth century, Irish and German immigrants settled in the area, together with nonimmigrant families of English descent. Shortly after, it attracted a sizable Slovenian population. The area became home to local foundries, and railroads were laid through the area, bringing a number of factories and other businesses founded by enterprising industrialists.

As with most melting pots, the area was complete with vibrant, if sometimes clashing, cultures. At the turn of the century, the area's population had grown to include Hungarians, Poles, Austrians, and Macedonians. By the First World War, African Americans had begun to move into the neighborhood. The vibrant, local cultures were best characterized by former Indianapolis mayor, Charles Boswell, himself a native of the near-west side, who said, "We got along with each other on all the days except when we fought—the fighting didn't take place more than five to six days a week."[3]

The neighborhood's booming industry was hit hard during the Great Depression. And while its economic condition improved during World War II, the economic boom after the war led many residents outside the community for more appealing and higher-paying jobs. Vacated houses were filled by lower-income white Appalachian workers and African Americans who had moved to the city to find work during the war. At the same time several large companies closed operations, their buildings were razed, and smaller, less lucrative businesses emerged in their place such as grocery and drug stores.

Perhaps more symbolically damaging to the area was the construction of a public-housing development on the site of one of the former large businesses. Poverty and crime rose, and the all-too-familiar urban downward spiral began. Important civic institutions such as firehouses, libraries, and schools that were as old as the neighborhoods closed, which created in residents a sense that their city had left them behind. A survey of neighborhood residents in the early 1970s indicated that apathy was a common problem and that productive outlets for youth and needed public services were severely lacking.[4]

Of the three neighborhoods, the WESCO neighborhood experience embodies key components of urban empowerment and warrants special attention as an individual case study, which forms a later section, "The Western Miracle."

## The Southeast Neighborhood

The southeast side of Indianapolis is one of the most historic communities in the city outside of the downtown district. Primarily a white neighborhood from the beginning, it was comprised of German and Irish immigrants who had joined others who had migrated from the East Coast and from several southern states.

The area enjoyed continuous commercial growth from the 1880s through the first three decades of the twentieth century. It became known as "Fountain Square," after a large fountain was erected in the center of its bustling commercial center. It was home to a variety of businesses, including clothing, furniture, and interior design enterprises, and between 1909 and 1929, eleven theaters were built in this relatively small part of town.

By 1950, African Americans composed only about 4 percent of the population, and poor Appalachian whites had moved into the community. During the 1950s, businesses began to take advantage of developments south of the city and moved out. All of the theaters closed down. And the fountain was even moved out of the commercial district, which had all but died, to a nearby park.

In the 1960s and 1970s the construction of the interchange for Interstates 65 and 70 displaced over 6,000 Fountain Square residents, which accounted for 25 percent of the area's population at that time. Almost all of the area's housing stock built between 1870 and 1910 was wiped out. Fountain Square has never fully recovered. The neighborhood was designated by the city in 1970 as a "special treatment" zone because of the disproportionate number of poor Appalachian white residents.

## Martindale-Brightwood

Martindale and Brightwood were founded as independent towns in the 1870s by workers in one of Indianapolis's busiest railroad hubs. Brightwood was founded by a mix of African Americans and European immigrants, most of whom worked for the Bee Railroad Line. The area quickly became the railroad center of Indianapolis. In 1880, 40 percent of the population was African-American. Martindale was founded by primarily African Americans who had found work in railroad-related machine shops and other manufacturers.

By the 1890s, Brightwood had started a high school, a private water works company, and two volunteer fire departments. Its business district remained the surrounding area's commercial center through the 1960s. One late-nineteenth-century observer described the town as "one big family" due to the fact that most families worked in the same shops and lived in neighborhoods that formed "a model city of cottages, in appearance resembling a large park."[5]

By the early twentieth century, Martindale had developed a diverse industrial mix, including a gas works company, an auto manufacturing firm, the Monon Railroad yards, a lumberyard, and several other factories. Residences and churches shared streets with businesses, and the community provided itself with a school, a park, and a public pool.

But in 1908 the railroad hub of Indianapolis moved south and west of Indianapolis, which initiated a slow exodus of workers in the railroad-related industries. Brightwood's railway station was demolished in 1944. By then, all of its railroad business had relocated. As suburbs expanded after World War II, attracting most of the area's white residents, low-income African Americans filled in the vacated houses, which began a trend that lasted through 1990.[6]

# The Challenge

The three decades prior to Goldsmith's election as mayor took their toll on the three neighborhoods, leaving their civic infrastructure exhausted. Population had declined 26 percent in the WESCO between 1960 and 1990, 46.6 percent in the SUMO area, and 56 percent in Martindale-Brightwood. The WESCO area saw its percentage of married women drop from 62 to 40 percent, and its number of married men drop from 67 to 44 percent. The SUMO area's marriage rate fell 62 to 49 percent for women, 67 to 48 percent for men. In Martindale-Brightwood, the numbers fell from 58.5 to 39.5 percent among women and from 64 to 39 percent among men.

In 1960, household income in the WESCO area was 95 percent of the median income for Indianapolis. In 1990, it was 59 percent, and 28 percent of all families were in poverty. In the SUMO area, similarly, the percentage of median household income dropped from 89 to 58 percent, with 28.5 percent of all families below the poverty line. In Martindale-Brightwood, the numbers fell from 75 to 53 percent, with 37 percent of families in poverty. Housing vacancy in Martindale-Brightwood also rose from 7 to 21 percent of all houses during this time. In all three neighborhoods the percentage of senior citizens rose considerably, and that of youth declined substantially. And each of the neighborhoods has seen the gap between its education levels and the rest of the city widen at a disconcerting rate.

The Goldsmith administration's Neighborhood Empowerment Initiative (NEI) was not announced as the solution to all of these problems. Rather, it was launched as a way to equip neighborhoods to play a more active role in defining solutions and executing plans to reach them. And the interviewees understood this. Most of them also recognized NEI's inherent virtue, namely the devolution of key decision-making to them, so that they could solve problems the way they knew was best for their community.

WESCO is a neighborhood association with roots dating back to 1974. It was a logical choice for the role of umbrella organization on the near-west side. The neighborhood also had an active community development corporation (CDC). Though WESCO and the CDC have remained distinct organizations with distinct boards, they both have their "fingers" deep into the community and only engage in projects for which they have wide-scale community support.

Olgen Williams, who was elected chairman of WESCO in 1993 when the NEI was first implemented, says, "On the near-west side, all of what we do is community enterprise. We don't favor certain ethnic, racial, or religious groups over others. We work with the CDC, they work with us, and any of the community-based organizations in the neighborhood that work with us understand that our business is community business." Mark Stokes, head of the CDC, remarks, "We are 100 percent a neighborhood organization. We don't do anything that doesn't somehow have its roots in what the residents of the neighborhood want and support."

This community-mindedness was more than an ideal but a mode of practice that drove the near-west side's success. It manifested itself in three important domains: *grassroots organization built on an extensive committee structure, strong leadership, and an emphasis on community involvement itself as much as running programs well.*

Committees and subcommittees were formed to carry out a number of programs and plans, as the case study in the next section will describe, creating a buzzing type of "grassroots federalism" in which residents attempted to drive key decision-making all the way down to the block level. Olgen Williams has nearly become a household name in Indianapolis for his grassroots leadership. Others in the community, from pastors to resident activists, also made names for themselves by inspiring initiatives that drove out drugs, increased programming for youth, and created jobs. And more than residents of the other neighborhoods, WESCO area interviewees talked as much about the process of neighborhood-based citizen engagement as any of the actual social outcomes that their programs achieved. They are proud of their ability to organize themselves, produce a lot of change with modest amounts of money, coordinate their activity with public officials, and uphold high standards of performance.

SUMO was formed by residents on the near-southeast side of the city after Goldsmith announced the requirement that neighborhoods form an umbrella organization in order to participate in NEI. The fact that SUMO was started "artificially"—meaning that it did not grow organically from a neighborhood association already at work in the neighborhood—created an interesting, if tension-filled, dynamic. The Southeast Neighborhood Development Corporation (SEND) is the southeast side's highly active and successful CDC, and it is not a member of SUMO. This has also created tensions in the neighborhood.

SUMO was formed in order to qualify for a neighborhood coordinator and for project funds, as stipulated by the administration. It did not develop the elaborate committee structure and "grassroots federalism" with which the WESCO area experimented, but began with several regularly scheduled community meetings: a code-compliance committee and a police task force. The residents also participated in the leadership-training workshops sponsored by the city.

SUMO residents conceive of their experience with empowerment in a substantially different way than WESCO residents. Two unique and significant characteristics marked the interviews as a whole. First, the interviewees possessed an uncanny preoccupation with property and the physical condition of the neighborhood. The SUMO area was marked by a disproportionately high number of property crimes and had too many absentee landlords who had allowed their properties to deteriorate into code violations, creating eyesores and safety hazards. The neighborhood has held the ignominious record for the highest death-by-fire rate in the city. Community leaders wanted their empowerment initiative to focus on property-related issues. Code-compliance efforts constitute a major piece of the empowerment pie in Fountain Square.

Second, SUMO residents felt notably "distant" from city hall. Their standard for "working together" with municipal government was much different than WESCO's. When they would cite instances of improved relations between local government and themselves, they usually focused on more frequent communication than in the past, but there were few examples of actual *collaboration*—which involves co-planning and building on mutual interests. Interviewees were greatly skeptical of government at all levels, and they seemed predisposed to believe that government initiatives were faulty, or even conspiratorial, from the start.

Many resident activists are old enough to remember the construction of the interstates. When they speak of being "cut off" from city hall and the rest of downtown, this is the visual image they invoke. They regularly said that the city wanted nothing to do with them, but there was in fact much investment in the area during the Goldsmith years.

The Indianapolis Economic Development Corporation assisted Anthem, the insurance giant, in its relocation onto a former nine-acre junkyard, which is now beautified and has expanded the southeast side of downtown. The Eli Lilly Corporation, in the northwest quadrant of the SUMO area, carried out a $1 billion expansion in 1999 and has created 7,500 new jobs. These efforts culminated in other business turnaround in the area, and the revitalization of the area paved the way for the Conseco Fieldhouse to be constructed on property adjacent to Anthem. A business incubator was launched in the area, and three manufacturing and distribution companies expanded during the 1990s. In an effort to invigorate an arts district in the heart of Fountain Square, SEND and the University of Indianapolis are converting an old warehouse into affordable studios and apartments for artists. Guaranteed low rents will offer security to artists even as property values rise around them. However, complained the residents, the city did not drive the investments into the heart of the neighborhood.

Whatever real or perceived "isolation" exists within the neighborhood, the SUMO area saw a greater rise in percentage of neighborhood associations during NEI than the other two neighborhoods, and it proved to be adept at drawing down Community Development Block Grant (CDBG) funds. While neighborhoods had trouble spending all of the $50,000 they each received annually from the city under NEI, SUMO consistently expended the majority—or all—of their allotted funds in a year.

Of the three neighborhoods in this study, Martindale-Brightwood had the hardest time converting NEI opportunities into success. Crime, overall, fell nearly as much as in the WESCO area (though several years later), neighborhood associations were formed, and unemployment dropped at a rate on par with the other neighborhoods. But other vulnerability indicators, such as welfare recipient levels and infant mortality rates, reveal a neighborhood experiencing great distress. Interviews painted a picture of dedicated neighborhood residents who, for reasons difficult to grasp, were not able to effect substantial change.

Like the SUMO area, residents identified deteriorating housing stock—and property in general—as a source of much crime and disinvestment, and they formed an active code-compliance committee. But the neighborhood has suffered from a general lack of sustained organizational capacity. Early in NEI, they formed a police task force, but no definitive community policing was established. Town hall meetings that began in 1993 to engage residents in strategic planning were discontinued without feedback to the city.

Residents recall the time as one in which it was difficult to generate enthusiasm for grassroots organization and action. Most of the activity generated through NEI and CDBG funding was put into the construction of New Ralston Estates, an attractive development of single-unit homes on land donated by the city. Smaller projects such as neighborhood cleanups, quilting classes for seniors, and park mural-painting projects for youth did not generate sustained future activity. In general, most socially redeeming work was disconnected from an overall strategic plan to sustain grassroots action and decision-making.

Unlike the other two neighborhoods, which could point to successes in the past tense, the interviews with Martindale-Brightwood residents were continually laced with such expressions as "we're starting to see change," "communication is now improving," "people are beginning to see possibilities," and so on. The late drop in crime, which peaked in 1997, and the late start to an effective use of CDBG funds indicate that perhaps the neighborhood is something of a late bloomer whose best days are ahead.

The neighborhood suffers from several setbacks in comparison to the other two. It has no sizable and well-funded community social service institutions, and its CDC was not formed until the time NEI was being started. Both the WESCO and SUMO areas had organizations within larger citywide social service networks and some history of CDC-based community development.

If the near-west side was marked by strong grassroots organization, leadership, and community involvement for its own sake, Martindale-Brightwood was marked by lower levels of organization, a faint grasp of what empowerment requires, and isolated examples of leadership. And, unlike SUMO, its umbrella organization, the Greater Citizens Coalition of Martindale-Brightwood, was not as successful at drawing down its allotted funding and securing other sources of funds.

Despite these setbacks, the area has been protected from further decline by the aggressive efforts of a number of city leaders. In the face of Martindale-Brightwood's deteriorating physical landscape and rising crime, five 100+ employee companies had begun plans to vacate the neighborhood between 1994 and 1998. They were persuaded to stay by city officials, resulting in 1,300 retained jobs and the creation of 120 new jobs. Had the companies left, it is difficult to predict how many others would have followed and created an economic vacuum from which economic recovery would have been nearly impossible.

Both SUMO and Martindale-Brightwood have perpetuated the spirit of NEI after Goldsmith left office by continuing to drive change initiatives through their umbrella organizations and in partnership with the city. After this study began, both were announced as sites by the Annie E. Casey Foundation for its Making Connections program, which aims to empower local leadership to drive urban reform. The Casey Foundation played a large part in helping the WESCO area organize itself early in the course of NEI. Hopefully, the continuing reforms in these two neighborhoods will create the kind of change that the WESCO area has experienced.

To gain a snapshot of successful empowerment, one only needs to visit the near-west side, or the WESCO area. The following section looks at the neighborhood's turnaround as a way to discover principles inherent to effective renewal of inner-city neighborhoods.

## The Western Miracle

The near-west side of Indianapolis has captured the national stage more than any Indianapolis neighborhood. Former U.S. Attorney General Janet Reno has visited the neighborhood, it has been the focus of a Department of Justice Best Practices study, and the Democratic Leadership Council's magazine, *Blue Print*, featured an article by WESCO's Olgen Williams on the Front Porch Alliance.[7] Any time there is a relatively rapid turnaround in a distressed urban community's condition, it seems miraculous given the odds.

The word *miracle* may be a bit misleading. It implies that a sudden, unplanned change occurred out of nowhere or in a manner contrary to what human reason would expect. The near-west side's success as a center of municipal citizenship did neither. Its ongoing revitalization is the result of strategy, investment, cooperation, leadership, and—perhaps most important—high levels of commitment. It is a miracle because it overcame the odds, but it did so in a way that is replicable elsewhere.

Community building efforts on the near-west side began nearly a year earlier than in the other neighborhoods. The WESCO area was in terrible shape in 1992. Not only had family breakup plagued the community, but the prolific amount of drug traffic and crime in the area gave the perpetrators control of the neighborhood. The drugs and crime were bad for business, evidenced by the continual flow of companies out of area, and they frightened residents, who preferred walling themselves into the safety of their own homes to involving themselves in community affairs.

### *Strengthening Grassroots Organization, Not Just Programs*

The city received a $190,000 planning grant from the Annie E. Casey Foundation for its targeted neighborhood strategy in 1993—a time when the Goldsmith administration was concentrating heavily on capacity-building strategies among neighborhood groups on the near-west side. During this period, its close working relationship with WESCO area leaders resulted in a Weed and Seed site designation from the U.S. Department of Justice in January 1993. Federal dollars began flowing into the neighborhood in 1995.

The Weed and Seed program focuses on effective law enforcement, community policing, prevention strategies, and neighborhood revitalization. The WESCO area took all aspects of the program seriously and has received national recognition as a result. Early in the process, under impressive grassroots leadership, the residents came to agreement that they were willing to work hard to clean up their neighborhood and create an environment that helped their youth flourish. During this process, the neighborhood held numerous meetings in which residents and public officials aired mutual concerns and strategized together. The mutual trust that developed between police and residents through this initial stage has led to the stuff of best practices.

The neighborhood also received $100,000 in initial seed money from the city compared to the $50,000 received by the other targeted neighborhoods, which enabled it to begin a broad array of activities. And while the amount of money is significant, what is perhaps more important is the neighborhood capacity to use the funds for the right purposes. Reverend Mel Jackson, a pastor well-known for strong community leadership, remarks:

> Strengthening the family unit should be the focal point of most of the activity in the neighborhood, and this needs to be done by the residents, grassroots groups, and the churches. Government should support that work however it can and be responsive in caring for more structural concerns like those that pertain to code-compliance enforcement. Funding for physical, structural improvements is very important, but only when resources are put directly into the neighborhoods in a way that builds up strong partnerships can there be long-term improvement.

Leaders on the near-west side embodied wisdom regarding funding. They generally agreed that resources were good for programming, but they were just as good for building up the human capacity to organize, cooperate, and live according to high standards. As Reverend Jackson points out, this begins with the family and must involve a willingness and ability to enter into socially redeeming partnerships. If these priorities are lost, then no matter how well other objectives are funded, failure will follow.

The initial Weed and Seed and NEI activities made something of an "organization" out of the neighborhood, so to speak, before any funds actually arrived. Administered by WESCO and the city, the initial planning process that began in 1992 gave birth to a proliferation of committees, each tasked with important neighborhood business. An executive committee, comprised of public officials and residents, identified problems and possible solutions, and then subcommittees were formed in which the residents were able to make the ultimate decisions about how a variety of policies—from crime to housing to social services—would be implemented.

A neighborhood governance subcommittee was formed that undertook the process of democratizing the entire effort on a human scale. In effect, grassroots federalism was at work. The subcommittee sought to more actively engage residents from every single block in the neighborhood. They designed a block-club system in which every block had a captain responsible for communicating between the subcommittee and the residents.

This was, in effect, an effort to create a local system of checks and balances within the neighborhood. Ultimately, the system never fully materialized, partly out of inefficient design and overly high expectations of volunteer residents. But it served to create a spirit of participation throughout the neighborhood. Perhaps this is why WESCO was the chief proponent among neighborhood groups of Goldsmith's Municipal Federalism initiative before the City-County Council struck it down.

The Weed and Seed process set the standard for future cooperation between city officials and WESCO area residents. Though they admitted to growing weary at times before the grant was actually awarded, they believed strongly in the citizen engagement it inspired. Every interviewee who was involved with a subsequent $3.5 million U.S. Department of Labor Youth Fair Chance grant, which helped the neighborhood send fifty-seven of its teenagers to college, complained that the grant was not suited to their unique circumstances because they did not have a say in the proposal process. As one former WESCO president remarked, the city "dropped it on the neighborhood. It's good to have the money, but it's not entirely tailored to our needs."

Their belief in up-front involvement in funding processes led the residents to active involvement in applying for and receiving a $30 million Hope VI grant for complete renovation of a public housing complex. Residents consider the grant, which came to the neighborhood owing to its demonstrated commitment to community renewal, a success because they were able to help government officials design how it would be spent.

The best way to exemplify the spirit of volunteerism that animates the near-west side is to point out that 120 people were on WESCO's social services committee soon after the city launched its empowerment initiatives. People were so energized about the prospect of being in control of their destiny, says Williams, that they started committing themselves to an abundance of meetings—perhaps "more than any neighborhood in the world," he jokes.

This may have become the case simply because the neighborhood had a lot to meet about. At first, priority was given to crime reduction and prevention. The Weed and Seed objective was crime reduction, but the way in which the grant proposal was drafted jump-started civic participation. Neighborhood residents participated in the proposal process and worked side-by-side with city officials to define the terms and conditions of the proposal. They determined the initiatives the neighborhood would undertake, how success would be defined, and so on. Williams calls the Weed and Seed process "*the* key to instilling a thirst for continued empowerment" among residents in the WESCO area. The money, which finally arrived nearly three years after the planning began, gave them the ability to take on a new experiment in community policing and resident-driven programming. But the planning process itself was just as valuable for defining the way in which they as a neighborhood would work together.

No grassroots organization process can succeed without leadership. Early in the city's empowerment efforts, Goldsmith brought Robert Woodson of the National Center for Neighborhood Enterprise to Indianapolis to conduct training sessions. Williams, who was elected WESCO's chairman in 1993, remembers having a "light-bulb experience" as he listened to Woodson talk about what empowered neighborhoods could look like. "Goldsmith came to us early on and said, 'We want you guys to take control of your neighborhood and tell us what to do to help you,' and Woodson's training helped us know how to do that, how to be in control of our neighborhood and in partnership with the city at the same time." More than in the other two neighborhoods, WESCO's residents remember the training supplied by Woodson as helpful in painting a picture of what sustained empowerment would look like.

One example of the results of high-impact community involvement is the case of infant mortality on the near-west side, which was at an epidemic scale before the neighborhood began turning around. Early in the near-west side's empowerment strategy, residents identified the unacceptably high levels of infant deaths in the neighborhood as a problem in need of an immediate solution. A lack of health education and practices among young mothers was identified as the root cause, and neighborhood leaders met the problem head-on. They created health-education classes for expectant and young mothers. They also established a strong relationship with a health clinic they had helped attract to the area in their early work with public officials. And because of their strong, block-based network of relationships, they were able to recruit mothers by word of mouth. The results are remarkable.

## Figure 1

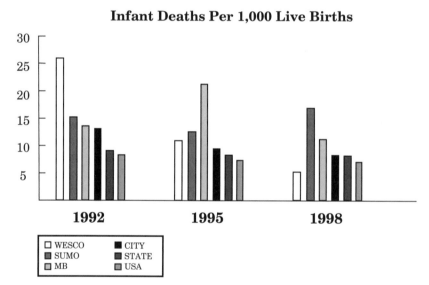

**Infant Deaths Per 1,000 Live Births**

Data compiled from "Health Vital Statistics," and "Vital Statistics," SAVI (1991-1998); and "National Vital Statistics Reports," National Center for Health Statistics.

Between 1992 and 1998, the national infant mortality rate dropped 16.3 percent, and it dropped 10 percent in the state of Indiana. In Indianapolis, it dropped 31.7 percent, and in the WESCO area as a whole, it plummeted 79.1 percent. Martindale-Brightwood saw a 12.6 percent drop, and only the southeast neighborhood experienced a rise, also 12.6 percent. As a percentage of all deaths, infant deaths dropped from 3.8 to .07 percent on the near-west side, while dropping slightly in Martindale-Brightwood and not at all on the southeast side. Indianapolis as a whole tackled its infant mortality problem after Goldsmith took office and is a remarkable story in itself, evidenced by the fact that its rate reduction was three times that of Indiana's and nearly double the national rate. All the more, the near-west side residents are an example of how implementing a grassroots approach of the most intensive variety can overcome a serious problem.

In the process, the neighborhood reduced its death per 1,000 births from 26.3 in 1992 to 5.5 in 1998. Not only is it remarkable for an inner-city neighborhood to experience such a dramatic turnaround, it is even more impressive that it undercut the national rate in 1998, 7.2, by nearly two points.

### Citizen Engagement as a Magnet for Success

Residents of the near-west side confirm that early successes helped instill a sensitivity in the neighborhood to "carrying the ball themselves." They learned that small wins were critical. Williams waxes philosophically about the nature of citizen engagement: "The biggest thing about empowerment is the people. They need to be attached to their neighborhood, and to be attached, they need to be inspired to know their voice matters. You have to have some successes early on that they can see that they had something to do with."

There was enough activity in the neighborhood to generate a diverse array of small-scale successes, such as the presence of new youth programming or a section of blocks that residents were aggressively keeping clean. Residents worked with the police department to identify abandoned vehicles, which resulted in 160 tagged and nearly 70 voluntarily removed cars—all by the end of the first year of NEI. They helped the police locate key crack-cocaine dealers who were subsequently arrested and prosecuted, worked with housing officials to improve the process for rehabilitating public housing, collaborated with workforce officials in establishing a one-stop job center in their neighborhood, and held community festivals that brought youth and adults together to draw attention to their accomplishments.

In short, citizen engagement on the near-west side made the neighborhood safer, infused it with meaningful volunteerism, attracted investment, and reinvigorated community spirit.

### Crime Reduction

All of this citizen activity paid off in terms of crime reduction. Drops in crime were seen all across the near-west side, but especially in the designated Weed and Seed areas of the neighborhood where community policing was in full force. But the success reached far more deeply than crime reduction. New relationships had formed. "Before Goldsmith's initiatives, we didn't know a single police officer's name," says Olgen Williams. "And now officers play kick ball with our kids, we honor them at an annual dinner. In the beginning, we had a lot of forgiving to do for past wrongs with the police, but now there's trust, there's a relationship."

Tyrone Chandler, the director of the Weed and Seed initiative in the neighborhood, writes about how far the relationship with police had come after several years of working together:

> Perhaps the strongest evidence of the change in police-community relations came in September 1998, when a drug dealer under surveillance emerged from his residence firing an AK-47 at police officers. The police returned fire and wounded the shooter. Almost immediately, rumors spread among those at the scene that white police officers had shot a young black man in the back five times. A local minister who was a community leader arrived at the scene. The Indianapolis police officers recognized the minister because they had worked together on other issues, and invited him behind the police crime-scene tape to hear what happened and see the bullet-riddled patrol car. He shared these facts with the crowd, which then dispersed without incident. Building on this positive experience, the chief plans to implement a . . . chaplaincy program proposed by the community that would train a pool of local ministers from each neighborhood to interact with police at crime scenes. The ministers would wear a special identification badge, assist IPD in communicating with local residents about sensitive and high-visibility incidents, and encourage those with any information to come forward.[8]

The relationship with the police is indicative of the manner in which WESCO area citizens and public officials of different sorts cooperate. Dianne Arnold, director of the Hawthorne Community Center, who proudly describes the near-west side as "an example of pure neighborhood-based empowerment," says that the WESCO area is "a model of partnership between the city and the neighborhoods." People got to know city officials so well, she said, that they "never hesitate to pick up the phone and call one of them for help on some issue or project. We learned what they were good at, what we were good at, and how we needed to work together to make our neighborhood a place where people would want to be."

Reverend Jackson concurs, "The neighborhoods now have a real working partnership with public officials, primarily from the mayor's office and its departments." This partnership, he adds, is the way politics should be at the community level. "The media and the political parties in town heighten negativity in politics and foster partisanship—they're divisive, they create distrust."

The willingness of WESCO area leaders to collaborate with public officials and their proven capability to organize themselves has attracted new partners and investment and has fostered a sense of community pride unknown in over thirty years.

### Volunteers and Partners

Surrounding institutions and corporations have noticed the expansive energy of the WESCO area residents and have begun to form partnerships with the neighborhood. Indiana-Purdue University at Indianapolis, which is the city's main academic institution with over 27,000 students and home to Indiana University's reputable business and medical schools, partnered with WESCO to form a tutoring program. More than thirty-five university students, ranging from undergraduate freshmen to medical students, come to the near-west side to tutor youth, conduct computer-training seminars, and provide activities for senior citizens. Rolls-Royce Allison Engine Company, located near the neighborhood's borders, created a partnership with the neighborhood in the summer of 2000 in which over 300 of the company's employees serve as mentors, tutors, and volunteers for community projects. The road to municipal citizenship on the near-west side was paved with small wins that have converted into big victories.

WESCO has more than sixty-five collaborations with public and private agencies, and the Christamore House, a neighborhood-based social services organization of which Williams is executive director, has scores of community partnerships and more than 100 regular volunteers.

### New Investment

Twenty-five new businesses, large and small, started in the neighborhood since NEI began, including several by members of Indianapolis's fast-growing Hispanic community. More than 1,000 jobs have been retained in the area, and nearly 150 new jobs were created between 1992 and 1996 in just four mid- to large-sized manufacturing companies in the area.

The city and the Indianapolis Economic Development Corporation worked with community development and business leaders in the neighborhood to redevelop an old twenty-two-acre rail yard into a complex for four sizable manufacturers and a vacated manufacturing facility into an office complex for several additional companies. The businesses include a medical-devices manufacturer, a machine and tool manufacturer, and a large cabinetry maker. Goodwill Industries, which had joined forces with WESCO to provide employment opportunities for area residents, also built a $1.6 million, 50,000 square-foot warehouse facility on the site. A 500-employee manufacturer was persuaded to remain in the area after the near-west side began to show signs of revitalization.

As an indication of how well people have found gainful employment, Williams says, the neighborhood has recently been unable to find anyone to participate in its "Hammer West" program, a jobs training and placement service for people facing multiple barriers to employment. What began with a program with 60 to 65 participants per class is without any takers today. "Everyone in our neighborhood who wants to work is working," says Williams.

### Community Spirit

What is the best measure of empowerment? Certainly the number of people who participate in community projects is a viable indicator. So are drops in crime numbers. But to Indianapolis police officer, Brad Thomas, the most significant indicator came at Christmas 1999. "We saw Christmas lights strung up all over the neighborhood, in people's windows, and on Christmas trees that families were proudly displaying. That was the first time we saw Christmas visibly celebrated this way." A trite measure? Not to Thomas, who claims that it is precisely this sort of activity that shows residents own their neighborhood like never before. More than this, a local grocery store manager reports seeing a sharp rise in sales in the past couple of years, and Williams reports that students are performing at historically high levels. In 1997 the neighborhood began having an award ceremony for honor roll students. Twelve students were recognized. At the conclusion of the school year in 2000, they honored more than 200 students from their community that had made the honor roll in their respective schools.

Arguably, the kind of organizing that took place on the near-west side was as important as the funds that paid for it. Indeed, it was the endgame for which the funds were initially deployed. The neighborhood's ability to organize itself paid off in many different ways. If the general picture painted in this chapter about the WESCO area seems overly optimistic and rosy, it was owing to the residents' confidence. This confidence is in turn based on the belief that if people are willing to work together, and they have the support of their government leaders, then progress will be made.

Former U.S. Attorney for the Indianapolis South District, Deborah Daniels, who headed up the initial Weed and Seed planning, describes the change in the WESCO area this way: "There was an overriding shift in attitude on the part of the people who lived in the neighborhood, from a very skeptical and suspicious attitude and the feeling they had no control over their destiny to a very strong sense of empowerment."

If no one else continues to speculate about the meaning of the neighborhood's success, Olgen Williams will. In the philosophical posture that he is wont to assume, Williams, an African-American Christian, says:

> We don't deal with politics, race, or religion in our neighborhood. I don't deal in minority business. I deal in neighborhood business, and if you are willing to work with us, I don't care if you're black, white, red, yellow, or blue, we'll sign you up and support you. If a neighborhood is going to experience empowerment, then people need to unify—not divide—themselves, and their leaders need to accomplish three things: forgiveness between people that have experienced wrongs, trust so that you can work together, and faith in God and in the belief that if you keep working together, you will succeed.

## Architecture for Empowerment

The experience with empowerment in Martindale-Brightwood, SUMO, and WESCO reveals several critical components to urban empowerment that should be unpacked and studied by anyone seeking to understand neighborhood-based urban renewal. These components have not been imposed on the study in advance. Rather, they emerged from the interviews with leaders of all three neighborhoods as the key elements without which the Goldsmith empowerment initiatives would have failed. City officials and other community leaders whom we interviewed repeatedly referenced them as well.

In short, the components are as follows:

**Crime Control**. The historically significant moment in WESCO came when residents, along with the rest of the city, saw drug dealers losing power in the neighborhood to the alliance formed between residents and the police department. The Martindale-Brightwood and SUMO neighborhoods concurred with WESCO, as will be shown later, that it is not merely the reduction in crime that empowers residents, but the *way in which* crime is addressed. Empowerment occurs when residents and police work together to make a neighborhood unfit for crime, on the one hand, and suitable for redeeming activities and practices, on the other.

**Citizen Involvement and Decision-Making Authority**. Clearly, the residents of the near-west side demonstrated a dramatic increase in civic participation. Volunteerism rose substantially, but this was not because of a newfound respect for altruism in the neighborhood. It rose because residents saw that active ownership of community affairs paid off. It benefited them, their children, and their neighbors. It made the neighborhood a better place to live and work. It resulted in increased services. And it placed on the residents the weight of responsibility, which is the mother of care and innovation. The other two neighborhoods also demonstrated that empowerment succeeds to the degree to which people are able to successfully organize themselves around a common purpose, develop leadership, and manage the responsibility of decision-making on behalf of the neighborhood.

**Financial and Material Resources**. The influx of capital, both in the form of public funds and private investment, together with improvements to housing and other physical structures, gives neighborhood residents a sense that they were moving forward. This is admittedly a broad category, but for the interviewees in the three neighborhoods, money, housing, and overall neighborhood condition were related and of a different nature than the other components of empowerment. The physical condition of the neighborhood is a direct reflection of quality of investment in the community. But it is also a reflection on the ability of residents to work together with public officials to eliminate abuses to property that discourage investment. Capital improvement and increased economic opportunity are essential to making empowerment work, but contrary to popular opinion, as the case of the three neighborhoods in this study will show, it is not the amount of capital but the manner in which it is used that makes the difference. A lot can be done with small grants and modest capital increases so long as they are rightly focused.

**Government-Community Partnership**. Almost every interviewee in the neighborhoods cited the Goldsmith administration's outreach as the ball that got empowerment rolling. But it did not stop with outreach. It picked up speed to the degree that city officials and neighborhood residents coordinated their activity to make the best use of the strengths each had to offer. The success of the near-west side is largely a function of the repetitive interaction between government and neighborhood and the manner in which decisions formerly reserved for government were shared—in a structural way, such as committees composed of both neighborhood leaders and government officials—with residents. Despite criticisms that interviewees had of the city, *not one person* criticized the city for the way in which it reached out and offered a genuine partnership to his or her neighborhood. In fact, most praised the city for it.

## Crime Control

The three neighborhoods in this study, like all of those targeted during the Goldsmith administration, had overly high levels of crime. This was compounded by the fact that crack cocaine infiltrated Indianapolis later than in other large cities, hitting its peak at the beginning of Goldsmith's tenure. Crack is infamous for causing escalations in violent crime. For instance, the percentage of arrested felons testing positive for crack in Indianapolis jumped from 22 percent in 1990 to 70 percent in 1994.

Empowerment among residents is completely undercut if crime is not under control, which explains the aggressive stance Goldsmith took on crime and the innovation that the police department undertook in the face of rising crime rates.

**Figure 2**

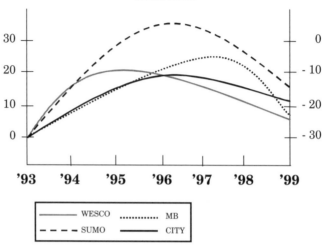

Percentage Increase and Decrease in Crime,
1993-1999

Crime statistics compiled from data supplied by the Indianapolis Police
Department Crime Analysis Unit, GIS.

Crimes peaked in the WESCO area in 1995. They peaked for the city
and the SUMO area in 1996, and for Martindale-Brightwood in 1997.
There were no increases in crime once the declines began. Martindale-
Brightwood experienced an increase of 23 percent between 1993 and its
peak in 1997, and then crimes dropped roughly 23 percent from 1997 to
1999. SUMO experienced an increase of 34 percent between 1993 and
its 1996 peak, before experiencing a 14 percent decrease between 1996
and 1999. Crime in WESCO increased 20 percent between 1993 and its
1995 peak, and then dropped 22 percent between 1995 and 1999.
Indianapolis as a whole saw crime rise 17 percent between 1993 and its
1996 peak, and then drop 18 percent between 1996 and 1999.

Between 1993 and 1999, the WESCO neighborhood saw a 7 percent
drop in overall crime, and Martindale-Brightwood experienced a 5 percent decline. Both of these neighborhoods outpaced the 4 percent drop
in crime citywide during this time. Only the SUMO area watched its
crime rate rise during this time. It increased 14 percent, despite its drop
after 1996.

*Principle One: Community policing works if approached with a
commitment to cooperate and think creatively.*

Figure 2 shows that by the mid-1990s, Indianapolis had begun to get crack and its overall crime problem under control. The near-west side, in particular, began driving its numbers down ahead of the city as a whole. But Figure 2 shows more. The peak times for crime in the three neighborhoods directly correspond with the critical mass that formed around empowerment initiatives in the respective neighborhoods. Funding for the Weed and Seed grant on the near-west side started in 1995, and community policing began full-force.

The Weed and Seed efforts, described earlier, were critical to kicking off the collaborative atmosphere between police and residents. This produced real results. The official Weed and Seed area only covered designated portions of the WESCO area, and in those areas since 1995, total crime fell 18 percent and property crime by 35 percent. Homicides decreased by 50 percent during this time—a period when they were climbing 19 percent in the rest of the city.[9]

In the SUMO area the new police substation was built in mid-1995, and by the fall of that year, a chief with a strong community policing impulse was hired for the area. Crime numbers began to fall at that point. Martindale-Brightwood is the general puzzler. When asked about the drop in crime rates, one longtime neighborhood activist exclaimed, "We have no idea—we never got community policing efforts to work. I speculate that criminals have decided to go elsewhere for now."

There was a general agreement among Martindale-Brightwood residents that community policing would be a good mechanism against crime, even though they had not mobilized themselves around the idea. The drop in crime for the neighborhood is attributable to several factors. One is that there were successful community policing efforts near the neighborhood that assisted in making the area unsuitable for would-be offenders. Another is that the citywide effort to aggressively attack the crack problem had gained full-scale momentum at that point and positively affected most of the neighborhoods around the Martindale-Brightwood area. But the worrisome point raised by the neighborhood leader quoted previously is that without the community policing infrastructure in place, she had no way of knowing whether or not crime would return. She and her neighbors were not in control of the situation.

*Principle Two: Crime is best countered when individual neighborhoods can customize their own crime-fighting strategy with the police and other public officials.*

Successful cooperation between residents and the police eventually pays off in terms of the new network of relationships that are formed.

A crime-fighting strategy that is rooted in a positive relationship between citizens and police only adds strength to the community in general. The near-west side has shown this to be the case not by design but by the natural outworking of open and honest collaboration. The residents organize award dinners for their police officers, and the police reciprocate by honoring neighborhood volunteers. In an effort to give a full range of decision-making authority to residents, the police department involves WESCO area neighbors in the hiring process of new officers for the neighborhood.

Before the aggressive approach to community-policing was implemented in the WESCO area, residents said they did not know the name of a single police officer. When they were given the opportunity to meet with the police during the early days of NEI, they expressed a strong desire for law and order, wanted the police to be tough on crime, and demanded that the "900 block of Concord," one of the worst drug-trafficking streets in the entire city, be cleaned up. They also engaged in a process of forgiveness, the residents said, in which they began to have faith in the possibility of improving police relations after years of an "us versus them" nonrelationship.

The district police chief began eating his lunch right in the middle of the 900 block of Concord after those meetings, and before long, officers were out of their squad cars—long the symbol of intrusive law enforcement—and walking the sidewalks, riding bikes, and even riding atop horses. They began to learn residents' names, and the residents began to feel comfortable calling on them for help.

It is impossible to separate this strong relational quality from the crime reductions in the WESCO area. Each interviewed officer and chief named the emphasis on relationship-building as the fundamental component to the overall crime-reduction effort. Residents reported feeling much safer since their relationships with the police improved, because they knew they were empowered to call on the police with the expectation of a timely response. The climate had changed so drastically, one interviewee said, that parents could let their children play outside without fear, and people could walk down the street "without having to look over their shoulders."

SUMO area residents may not be familiar with James Q. Wilson and George Kelling's "broken window" thesis but they articulate it beautifully.[10] The most important deterrent to crime, interviewees said, is to keep property in good shape and keep the streets clean. With shoddy and unkempt buildings lining the streets, crime is welcome in the community. "I equate trash with crime," argues one long-time activist, Richard Campi. "There is a direct link." A shabby environment must be combated head-on in order to prevent other crime.

SUMO residents had real concerns on this point. Not only do property crimes represent a larger share of overall crime in the SUMO area than the other neighborhoods, southeast side residents watched the number of violent crimes increase in recent years.[11] For this reason, they were generally satisfied that a stronger police presence in their community was having positive effects. The Indianapolis Police Department opened a new office in the center of the neighborhood's commercial district.

This was an intentional move by the Goldsmith administration to place the police in the center of the community and thereby facilitate more intentional and regular interaction with residents. One officer said that closer collaboration with community groups—in the form of meetings in which residents work with officers to identify criminals and agree on problem areas to address—was responsible for a 19 percent reduction in crime between 1997 and 1999 in two of the neighborhood's trouble zones.

Juanita Smith, a longtime neighborhood activist in Martindale-Brightwood remarks, "The key to empowerment is safety." She says that people will be empowered when they "feel secure with the police presence," and cites an incident in which a person who reported a crime experienced retaliation from friends of the accused. The lack of a cooperative, crime-fighting strategy in Martindale-Brightwood created a general lack of ease among residents despite the fact that they had experienced a significant drop in crime since 1997. In short, they did not feel empowered in the face of possible future crime.

### Citizen Involvement and Decision-Making Authority

At the same time a neighborhood is securing peace through its crime-fighting initiatives, it needs to be creating an atmosphere for positive citizen action. Community policing helps in this regard, but of course, it cannot and should not be the lone point of action for an engaged citizenry. As Goldsmith has articulated in this book, his administration's goal was to build a structure within which residents could make their voices heard and assume real responsibility over neighborhood affairs and services.

Three principles emerged from interviews regarding the NEI effort to place greater responsibility and oversight of programming into the hands of residents.

*Principle One: Residents want to have a greater say in decisions that affect them, and the stakes of civic engagement should be raised so that greater responsibility among them is expected and supported by the city.*

SUMO president Rachel Cooper remarks that "there was no empowerment until [Goldsmith's] administration came." The reason? Because, she says, he "opened the lines of communication between city hall and the neighborhoods for the first time." There was a general agreement among interviewees from all three neighborhoods that city hall's efforts to reach out to the neighborhoods was progress, because it empowered previously unheard citizens to speak and find an audience. One interviewee remarked that the date on which input from neighborhoods truly became possible was the day that NEI began.

The way that neighborhoods were required to make their voices heard was important. Goldsmith pointed out earlier that a revitalization of neighborhood associations was a deliberate attempt by his administration to create a more "Toquevillian" climate in Indianapolis. Residents were exhorted to organize themselves in associations and make demands on city hall—and they did.

Charlene Hedrick, the NEI director throughout Goldsmith's two terms as mayor, smiles as she remembers his method of energizing neighborhood leaders: "One of the most remarkable things about the mayor's efforts was simply that when he said to residents, 'Organize yourselves and picket me,' he was entirely serious. He meant it, and he meant it passionately, even though many of us in city hall were hoping people wouldn't take him seriously!" Even when they were not picketing, residents did take Goldsmith seriously. Former Deputy Mayor John Hall explains that "when residents came to city hall and demanded services, we knew they had graduated and understood the game." Former Front Porch Alliance Director Isaac Randolph says, "The Goldsmith administration measured success by the number of people it could help get involved in their communities."

Almost without exception, and despite any criticism they might have held for the mayoral administration, residents in all three neighborhoods heralded the mayor's push to mobilize associations. One neighborhood leader said, "Forcing us to get our act together and form neighborhood organizations is the best thing Goldsmith ever did." Another remarked, "By offering to work with us if we would form neighborhood organizations, the mayor gave us reason to care about our neighborhoods in a new way and like we never had before." And a southeast side resident put it this way: "The empowerment initiative 'put a face' on our neighborhood that it had never had since the Interstates tore it up three decades ago."

"One of the great things that Goldsmith did was really push neighborhood organizations as the best voice of the people," said one community organization leader, who made it clear that he was not usually a supporter of Goldsmith's policies. Neighborhood associations, another said, have an enhanced ability (over the individual) to call on someone in city government and actually get something productive done as a result. Not only this, but the confidence instilled in residents by open lines of communication created even more reasons to chart courses for neighborhood action on a number of fronts. Equally important as new lines of communication with city hall was the way that former walls between residents began to crumble. People began to see the value of common concerns as rallying points around which to organize action and get the city involved making grassroots efforts come alive.

During the Goldsmith administration, the number of registered neighborhood organizations in Indianapolis grew from 218 in 1991 to 520 at the end of 1999. The degree to which the residents are organized into associations and coalitions is another key indicator of empowerment activity in a neighborhood. Without neighborhood associations, positive action is much more difficult to coordinate, and if it does occur, it is usually because of a few people that hold most of the power (and resources).

Neighborhood associations are a valuable means to mobilizing a broad range of citizens on behalf of their shared interest and common good. By enabling many people to be involved in community affairs, they are also an important democratic mechanism that prevents power from concentrating in one or two hands. Of the more than 300 additional neighborhood associations to become officially registered during Goldsmith's tenure, some were created as residents organized themselves to respond to the conditions the city placed on them to make formal requests of the city and to be able to receive funds for their efforts. Others formed from loose neighborhood groups that already had a history of organizing neighborhood activities but had never officially established themselves. Each of the three neighborhoods considered in this study experienced an increase, with SUMO's being the greatest.

Between 1991 and 1999, the number of neighborhood associations grew from four to six in Martindale-Brightwood, seven to fourteen on the southeast side, and three to five on the near-west side.[12] Two points are in order. First, these numbers do not tell the whole story about a neighborhood's increased capacity for action, though they do indicate an increase in "social capital," understood as social networks that cultivate reciprocity and norms of trustworthiness.[13] These numbers cannot tell us how well the increase in organizations has leveraged additional resources for the neighborhood, and they do not show us the degree to which they have increased volunteerism in the neighborhoods.

While no inventory has been taken of the volunteerism generated by these groups, an analysis of the funding they drew into their neighborhoods, as the following section shows, indicates that they have been successful in increasing socially beneficial activity in their communities.

And, all anecdotal evidence suggests that the increase in organizations has been met by an even more significant increase in the number of volunteers and funds available to these neighborhoods.

While the presence of more groups generally means more competition for funds, it also means that other community partners formerly uninterested in the neighborhoods now consider them viable collaborators. Public agencies, for one, have demonstrated a willingness to work with neighborhood groups in a way unlike the past, and corporations are reaching out as well. The Eli Lilly Corporation, one of the nation's most formidable pharmaceutical corporations, has worked with neighborhood groups in the SUMO area, and, as I mentioned earlier, Rolls-Royce Allison has begun an aggressive community outreach program in the WESCO area. Without the increase in neighborhood organizations, these types of partnerships are less likely, because partners of this magnitude are unlikely to invest in community outreach without an *organization* with whom to partner.

The second point is that the registered associations in a neighborhood are not the only nonprofit community assets that have increased in these neighborhoods. Other kinds of private social service organizations such as private day care centers, elderly assistance organizations, learning centers, and health organizations, also provide help to the neighborhoods. By the end of 1999, Martindale-Brightwood had forty such organizations despite its lack of a large networked social service agency, the SUMO area had thirty-six, and WESCO, twenty-one.[14]

These figures do not include churches or other houses of worship, though they include several faith-based service providers. The number of churches in the neighborhoods did not change much during the Goldsmith administration, and even if it had, it would not be directly related to any of the administration's policies. The number of churches bears mention, however, to give a more complete picture of the nature of the grassroots activity in the neighborhoods. Between 1990 and 1999, the number of churches in Martindale-Brightwood rose from ninety-four to ninety-seven, more than fifty of which are Missionary Baptist churches and fourteen of which are Pentecostal. The remaining congregations are a variety of other forms of non-mainline Protestant churches. In SUMO the number of congregations dropped from thirty-nine to thirty-three between 1990 and 1999, and they include a diverse mixture of mainline and non-mainline Protestant churches and one Catholic church. In WESCO there is perhaps the most diverse set of churches ranging across all denominational lines including a Catholic and an Eastern Orthodox church, though the majority of congregations are non-mainline Protestant. The number of congregations in that neighborhood rose from forty-eight to sixty between 1990 and 1999, the most significant change of the three neighborhoods.[15] The Front Porch Alliance, Goldsmith's initiative to reach out to faith-based organizations, was active with churches from each of the three neighborhoods.

Raising the stakes of responsibility in the neighborhoods was effected by requiring that neighborhood organizations be the points of contact for the city. An increased number of neighborhood organizations increases the opportunity for neighborhood-based action, but they also create a greater number of organized interests in neighborhoods with the ability to communicate to local government. Rachel Cooper describes the city's requirement that residents organize their interests as "the big issue." She continues, "We have told the city, we're never going back to the way we were before the empowerment initiative."

*Principle Two: The requirement of umbrella organizations is widely viewed as a successful mechanism for uniting neighborhood activity around common goals and providing a single management structure.*

One WESCO area resident said that "empowerment is simply when the government makes money and technical assistance available and gets out of the way to let residents do the work." This rather sanguine portrayal of laissez-faire empowerment understates the important role that the local government plays in equipping residents to manage their own affairs, but it also betrays the level of confidence WESCO residents had in themselves. The umbrella organization was the mechanism through which residents would "do the work," and there was general agreement among interviewees that it was needed to empower neighborhoods. The umbrella organization strategy placed a premium on citizen engagement and made it easier to become engaged. "If you want to get involved," one resident said, "you can, because the structure is there."

One positive outcome of the umbrella-organization strategy was that it forced neighborhood residents—and other organizations within the same neighborhood—to work together, "something we'd never done before," in the words of one southeast resident. Linda Mintor, neighborhood coordinator for Martindale-Brightwood, says that the main objective in the neighborhood is to help residents "understand that without them, there is no city." The umbrella organization enables them to have a single place through which residents can decide how they are going to govern their own corner of the city. Though Martindale-Brightwood has struggled to get organized, the umbrella organization is the means by which funding and project ideas come together and provides the single point of contact for public officials. Citing a recent project meeting organized by the umbrella organization, Mintor says, "the residents were impressed at what they could get done" by uniting their concerns and committing to carry out a strategic plan with the city.

Yvonne Margendant, neighborhood coordinator for SUMO, attributes the neighborhood's success in closing twenty-seven drug houses to its newfound capacity for working collectively. Margendant also notes that there is undoubtedly a wider group of people today with more of a say in determining how grants are to be spent and how the division of labor on community projects is to be allocated than in previous years. The neighborhood has undertaken over twenty projects with CDBG funds, mainly focused on youth programming and green-space rehabilitation. Particularly with the latter case, she says, residents felt for the first time that they could directly counter the ill effects of the interstates to which they commonly look as the cause of their community problems and unattractive environment.

Of course, an umbrella organization itself does not work wonders. At least two factors determine its level of impact: the degree to which it represents the *neighborhood as a whole* and the degree to which its projects build a *series of "wins"* over real problems.

A common complaint in the SUMO area was that the umbrella organization did not take into account the *entire* community's interests. Cooperation, one community-based organization leader said, was usually a casualty of "balkanized squabbles" between the different neighborhood associations as they clamored for funding and position within SUMO. A director of a well-known organization in the area said that the board of SEND, the CDC for the area, was more representative of the neighborhood as a whole than the umbrella organization's board. This, he said, had decreased the confidence residents had in the umbrella organization's ability to produce long-term change in the community.

Another agreed that the umbrella organization was not "democratic" enough in the way it selects board members and was thus not positioned to make decisions representative of the neighborhood as a whole and administer resources in a fair and honest way.

WESCO's committee structure and strong leadership enabled the neighborhood to build a sustainable set of projects and create enough small "wins" to inspire future resident engagement. WESCO has made it a priority to develop the capacity in their neighborhood residents to be self-governing in a strict Toquevillian sense. They invested the grants they received in human services to the widest extent possible, because, as Olgen Williams says, "we wanted to build human capacity, not just have better bricks and mortar."

The neighborhood's preoccupation with having an extensive array of social services is built on the idea that not only do these services improve the quality of life of real people, they also equip people to take ownership of their community's fate. It enabled them to solve real, pressing social problems—such as the infant mortality problem described earlier—at the same time they were building neighborhood capacity to address future neighborhood concerns.

*Principle Three: The way leadership is defined and understood within the neighborhoods by the residents is as important as any particular initiatives and programs.*

"More people have gotten involved, but they don't seem to have gotten more power to change things." These words by one southeast side neighborhood leaders reflect a problem the SUMO area was having with leadership. The neighborhood may have birthed new neighborhood associations under NEI, but it did not have the experience with leadership that WESCO did. Unlike the leadership ethos on the near-west side, which Williams described as the task of guiding community business without favoring one group over another, the SUMO area's proliferation of neighborhood associations was not guided by a unifying project that benefited the whole neighborhood. Steve Scott, who was actively involved in a number of neighborhoods as a housing developer, describes the difference between well-led and poorly led neighborhoods as the way that the residents' vision is united and carried out: "In successful examples, residents as a whole supply the vision, and a well-connected and committed board carries out that vision." This is the difference between simply having more organizations and having more authority to change the way things work in a neighborhood.

Robert Hawthorne, former director of the Martindale-Brightwood CDC, says that "good leadership is the most important thing for neighborhood empowerment—the rest can be figured out when that's in place." But, he also said, in his neighborhood, people may have more "say-so in the neighborhood in the past few years, but say-so over what?" Residents from Martindale-Brightwood received training from the National Center for Neighborhood Enterprise, just as near-west side leaders did, but this alone did not build capacity to provide the "what" over which leadership could be exercised. That needs to be defined within the neighborhood by the residents themselves.

One Martindale-Brightwood resident remarked that no visibly long-lasting changes had been created within the neighborhood other than physical infrastructure improvements. Only leadership can unify a long-term effort. Nowhere is this more evident than in the way the neighborhood procured CDBG funds (which will be discussed more fully in the next section). Martindale-Brightwood was two years behind the other two neighborhoods in drawing down funding for community-based projects. Ultimately, it only funded two projects, both of which ended without creating any additional future programming. And while the other two neighborhoods had been successful in securing more than $400,000 each in CDBG funds already in 1994, Martindale-Brightwood only crossed the $200,000 mark for the first time in 1996. Not surprisingly, interviewees from this neighborhood complained of a lack of funding much more frequently than those from the other two neighborhoods.

Leadership training, such as that provided by Robert Woodson and his colleagues, made the time required "to draft bylaws, hold meetings, and write proposals worth it," said one WESCO resident. This cannot be understated. According to John Hall, the city invested $5 million in leadership training, by-laws education, proposal writing, and organizational management. More than any technicalities that they learned during the training, near-west side residents valued the training because it put flesh on the idea of empowerment. Woodson inspired them to believe they could take greater control of their future, and the fact that their city administration—not a private foundation or university—had brought him to do the training gave them the confidence that whatever they invested in leadership development would pay off because the city would respect the outcomes.

But once the training was finished, it is widely acknowledged that change was sustained over time particularly by Olgen Williams's practice of upholding high standards for the neighborhood, the city, and any neighborhood partners, together with his commitment to mobilizing groups of people around clearly identified projects. This kind of leadership, city officials and other community leaders repeatedly said in interviews, is absolutely necessary if empowerment is to be a success.

### Financial and Material Resources

An examination of the three neighborhoods considered here cannot be disconnected from initiatives aimed at improving economic opportunities citywide. The general efforts in Indianapolis to reduce welfare rolls and strengthen the economy benefited the three neighborhoods.

Like most states in America, Indiana has experienced a significant decline in the number of people receiving public assistance due to implementation of the 1996 federal welfare reform act. In Indianapolis, the number of families on welfare dropped 54.5 percent between 1994 and 1999, a remarkable decline well ahead of the 40.5 percent national urban average.[16]

The neighborhoods in this study also experienced a drop in the number of families receiving public assistance. Between 1997 and 1999, the years of the Goldsmith administration in which the new form of work-oriented public assistance, Temporary Assistance to Needy Families, was in effect, welfare rolls dropped in the three neighborhoods in a way consistent with the level of economic opportunity in each. The near-west side, where economic opportunity was at the greatest, saw a drop of 15.5 percent, the SUMO area 5.9 percent, and Martindale-Brightwood, 0.9 percent. For Indianapolis as a whole, there was a 31 percent drop.

Of course, the drop in welfare rolls means nothing if people are not finding sustainable employment.

Between 1992 and 1999, household income in each of the neighborhoods considered as a percentage of the Indianapolis median income crept upward—a promising development, considering it had been in steady decline in each of the neighborhoods since 1960. And the unemployment rates fell faster than the national rate, only slightly less than the citywide rate, and faster than the rate for central cities nationwide (see Figure 3).[17]

Median income inched upward between 0.6 and 0.7 percent in each of the neighborhoods. At least 2,000 jobs were retained and 1,000 created in companies that either were not in the neighborhoods in 1992 or had considered leaving during the 1990s but were persuaded otherwise by city officials.[18] This is no small point, given that the total labor force in the three neighborhoods is approximately 16,500 (although, of course, not all of the 3,000 jobs retained and created are held by neighborhood residents). Also, home-improvement loans increased in each neighborhood between 1994 and 1997, when empowerment initiatives were in full gear, indicating that investments by homeowners in their property were on the rise.

Compared to the city's distressed neighborhoods as a whole, whose unemployment rates are at about 9 percent, SUMO and Martindale-Brightwood are performing above average and WESCO is doing particularly well.

**Figure 3**

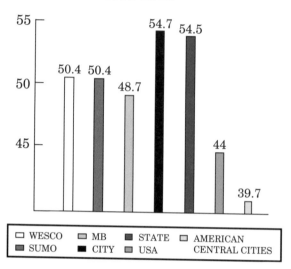

## Percentage Decline in Unemployment, 1992-1999

U.S. Bureau of Labor Statistics, U.S. Housing and Urban Development, and Indiana Department of Workforce Development. The 39.7 percent drop for central cities comes from HUD's "The Time Is Now: Places Left Behind in the New Economy" and is for 1992-1998.

The employment-creation initiatives carried out by the Goldsmith administration helped provide these favorable economic conditions for families. Additional resources are important for the community as a whole, either directly for programs that the neighborhood manages or in physical infrastructure. Earlier in this book, Goldsmith characterized the city's approach to funding as an effort to build the capacity of neighborhoods to be more self-determining. Physical infrastructure improvements are a necessary precursor to this type of empowerment. Interviews with residents confirmed the wisdom of this approach and helped paint a picture of how it plays out in real communities. Three principles bear mentioning.

*Principle One: City officials can and should creatively and competitively devolve community-building funds to a diverse group of local organizations rather than to a few preferred organizations.*

During Goldsmith's eight years in office, $80 million in CDBG funds were invested in community projects, many of them grassroots empowerment initiatives. The federal CDBG program is a U.S.

Department of Housing and Urban Development program that gives cities a considerable degree of latitude in deciding how the money is spent. By 1992, over 50 percent of CDBG funds in America were used on neighborhood-based "bricks and mortar" revitalization strategies, even though CDBG regulations do not require such a focused investment strategy.[19]

The trend toward a community-based urban development strategy was helped along in the 1980s by the sudden growth of CDCs, which concentrate rehabilitation efforts in specific geographic areas. CDCs mainly focus on property repair, rehabilitation, and development. Indianapolis took this trend a step further, beginning in 1993, by targeting CDBG funds not only to CDCs in a concentrated way but also to neighborhood associations. This devolution of responsibility over the administration of community-building funds naturally drives decision-making about community improvement to the grassroots level.

In 1993 there were just seven grants distributed to three organizations in the three neighborhoods for a total of $242,000. In 1999 there were thirty-six grants disbursed to eleven organizations for a total of $1,019,000. Funds were awarded on a competitive basis and only given to those capable of sound accounting practices and able to demonstrate results. Of these organizations, some were small, community-based organizations that are, in most cities, never offered a chance to bid for CDBG funds.

In most cases these grants leveraged significant amounts of additional public and private investments, the scope of which is difficult to assess but can safely be estimated at more than $200 million in the three neighborhoods between 1993 and 1999.[20] This is, in part, a product of the improved capacity within the neighborhoods for applying for and securing available funding. In 1993 the three neighborhoods accounted for slightly less than 3 percent of the approximately $9 million total CDBG disbursements made by the city, and in 1997 they accounted for slightly more than 7 percent of the approximately $13.8 million total.[21]

And in every case, accountability was the standard. One near-west side resident said that Goldsmith "made you account for every dollar you were planning on getting from him, but then he kept every promise he made and expected you to do the same."

It does not take much money to begin paving the road to empowerment. SUMO's board members all agreed that an initial $8,000 grant with which they improved several area parks and basketball courts, was enough to solidify them as an organization. The money enabled them to rally volunteers, pay for supplies, do the planning, and finish the work. At the end of the process they had begun to see the neighborhood change. For once, "we were able to work together and point to something that was ours, something that would not have been done without our mutual effort," one of them remarks.

Like the federal Weed and Seed grant program, which has achieved remarkable results without massive investment (the program is a $41 million project nationwide), the CDBG distributions under NEI in Indianapolis focused resources on specific and effective programs. The education that reduced the near-west side's infant mortality rate was a minimal-cost project. The cost of building trust between police and residents also does not cost much, and as the near-west side shows, the results are substantial.

*Principle Two: Improvement in the physical infrastructure is a valuable demonstration of concern for citizens' safety and sense of community.*

The link between well-maintained property and civic engagement was prevalent among interviewees. One resident said that the physical improvements in the neighborhood had renewed a sense among residents that revitalization is underway. Another remarked that physical improvements were returning the neighborhood to the 1950s, when it was stronger and marked by a greater level of interest in community affairs.

Bill Taft, executive director of SEND, the SUMO area's CDC, claims that city investments and other public and private investments in the overall physical infrastructure have led to a 75 percent increase in property values on the southeast side. More than this, he says, the neighborhood is gaining a unique identity again as a desirable place to be. Ken Gall, a community organization leader, described the neighborhood this way: "There's an increase in homeownership. There is a significant physical improvement to the properties and the neighborhood as a whole. There is a renewed attention to code enforcement." Though far from perfect, he said, these changes create a deeper sense among people that progress is possible and that the neighborhood does not need to be stuck in despair.

Residents in all three neighborhoods were very aware of the city's Building Better Neighborhoods program and were appreciative of the improvements that resulted to their communities. The southeast side's Yvonne Margendant says, "I don't even want to try to imagine what this neighborhood's sidewalks and buildings would look like today if the city had not rebuilt our infrastructure."

One longtime Martindale-Brightwood resident says she had "seen homeownership decline from over 80 percent to under 50 percent over the years" in her community and watched the neighborhood become the worse for it—which is why another neighborhood leader described a "sense of moving forward" when several decaying houses—neighborhood eyesores—were torn down.

All three neighborhoods closely associated housing and infrastructure decay as an invitation to criminal behavior. For this reason, each neighborhood has continued to have an active code-compliance committee. Residents overwhelmingly supported strong enforcement of their compliance recommendations. "We keep a running list of twenty-five code violators," says Martindale-Brightwood community leader, Shirley Webster, "and while we always gently contact them first, we stay on them and bring in the city when we have to. Believe me, we *know* our contacts at the city and they know us, because when it comes to keeping up to code, our safety and sense of community depends on it!"

If the practices of the three neighborhoods are any indication, code-compliance committees provide an urban community with one of the strongest vehicles for joint action that produces real results over which they feel ownership. "Broken windows" is not a theoretical expression for them: it is a daily reality over which they thirst for control.

*Principle Three: Residents have to be given the opportunity to draft proposals for funding at all levels and to feel that all funding efforts will equip them—and not someone else's agenda—to succeed.*

This point was made clearly in the previous case study on the WESCO area and does not need to be belabored here. WESCO leaders were unanimously disappointed that they did not have a say in the way that the Youth Fair Chance proposal was written. Contrariwise, eight years after the Weed and Seed process began, they continued to talk about it as a historically important moment for the neighborhood.

Residents in the other neighborhoods confirmed that they would rather take the time to involve themselves in the planning process for a grant—and participate in writing it—than simply receive money for something they cannot adapt well to their needs. It should be added that their degree of interest on this front was directly related to the degree that they considered their contacts at city hall to be accessible and helpful. Southeast side community leader, Elaine Cates, expresses a great deal of interest in working with public officials to secure resources because "they always get us hooked up with what we need or find out from someone else how we can [get what we need]."

What cannot be underestimated is the degree to which residents want to have control over funds they receive. They often care about this as much, or more, than the receipt of funds themselves. "While many good city initiatives have focused on capital improvements and economic empowerment," says a director of a local housing-rehabilitation nonprofit group, "unless people are empowered to take advantage of such improvements, then there's a big mismatch in a community." Residents in the three neighborhoods were no less desirous of money than other people are, but they demonstrated a remarkably sophisticated understanding of the need for participation, organizational capacity, and civic engagement to ensure that funds were employed in a way that enabled them to design real solutions to problems they faced.

### Government-Community Partnership

An Indiana University survey of Indianapolis's urban neighborhoods conducted at the end of Goldsmith's first term showed a 16 percent increase between 1993 and 1995 in positive responses to the question, "Is local government concerned about your neighborhood?" The same survey also revealed an 11 percent increase in the awareness urban residents had of organizations within their neighborhoods that dealt with neighborhood problems.

Martindale-Brightwood's Shirley Webster describes the empowerment process in the 1990s this way: "We went from being a partially empowered neighborhood to a knowledgeable community." This was due to the city's outreach and overall effort to supply neighborhoods with helpful information and resources through neighborhood coordinators, township administrators, town hall meetings, specialized training, and the Indianapolis Neighborhood Resource Center.

A generally improved attitude, one resident said, can be sensed in her neighborhood because it is more organized and the city has been more responsive to its needs. In previous years, interviewees said, they never felt connected to their public officials, but had come to feel as though the communication lines were up and running by the end of the 1990s. This alone has empowered them to create change by taking advantage of those open lines to get needed information or to ask someone within government for help. Citizens, an elderly resident says, will only be empowered "when they feel like someone cares." Not only had the city demonstrated more "care" in the 1990s than in the past, it continued to improve its outreach as time went on.

*Principle One: Establishing an official mechanism for residents to be in regular contact and conversation with public officials is critical.*

"One of the best things [Goldsmith] did was hire township administrators," one resident remarks, because they provide a link to city hall and help the residents navigate through complicated public documents and regulations. More than this, outreach by city hall helps break down long-standing walls between the community and municipal government. These walls are more than barriers to understanding. They are barriers to problem solving. The camps on either side of the walls often have a different grasp of problems facing the community and what needs to be done to tackle them.

For this reason, residents also saw the work of their neighborhood coordinators as indispensable. The coordinator, as well as the township administrator, helps open the door to an enlarged understanding of a problem and an enlarged grasp of possible solutions. Having someone who can speak the "language of government" and the "language of the neighborhood" is fundamentally important. This bilingual capability helps navigate residents through mazes of acronyms and agencies when they are applying for grants and coping with bureaucracy.

*Principle Two: The willingness to listen to residents and change plans to meet their concerns must be authentic if a long-term working relationship with them is to be established.*

A WESCO area leader said, "The city listens more attentively to the needs of the people than in the past," and that the most dramatic positive change "during the 1990s was the access that we had to the 25th floor of the city-county building (the mayor's office)."

Another near-west side organization leader held the neighborhood to be a successful model of public-private partnership because everyone in the city and the neighborhood took the time to assess—and agree on—their respective skills and contributions. This created a working relationship in which all the parties were able to be nimble in responding to immediate problems because a basic "division of labor" had been established in advance.

In the interviews, city officials communicated a shared sensibility about working with WESCO: it would be utterly foolish, they agreed, to devise a public initiative that affected the neighborhood without having the neighborhood leaders at the table from the start. Lieutenant Don Bender of the police department's west office says, "The city started listening to the neighborhood leaders instead of just listening to City-County Councilors. Instead, they go straight to the residents and ask, 'How do you want that done?'"

Not only would neighborhood participation improve a city initiative, the public officials learned, they knew they would have a band of angry residents on their hands if they did not include them as partners. So standard a procedure had the consultation of residents become that even state and federal law-enforcement officials began showing up at neighborhood meetings on the near-west side. They had learned that this was the way to do business in that part of town.

The change on the part of the city toward constant communication and listening was noticeable to residents. One west-side resident—echoing Lieutenant Bender—said, "Change really started happening when the City started listening to its residents." Near west-side residents commonly attributed the overall success of Goldsmith's empowerment initiatives to the frequency and quality of communication. One of the interviewees claims that the city officials were "great in every sense of the word" because they came out to the neighborhood to see firsthand what the problems were, connected residents to job networks, and helped residents discover skills that they did not realize they had.

What is interesting is the silence of residents on Goldsmith's accomplishments in government reforms such as the cost-cutting achieved through competitive services that have won him so much acclaim in the national media; for residents, what matters is what they can see in their own community, and what the residents of the near-west side saw was an administration that was sincere in its outreach and honest in the promises it made.

## Faith in the City: The Role of Faith in the Public Square

Goldsmith has explained the importance and challenge of partnering with the faith community in Chapters Four and Seven. Our interviews with residents revealed that the Indianapolis experience with FPA still permeates community leaders' minds. Everyone, it seemed, had an opinion about FPA. It was the capstone of the administration's attempt to build a working relationship with neighborhoods and thus warrants additional mention here.

FPA was active in the WESCO and Martindale-Brightwood areas. Residents from these two neighborhoods were favorable to the city's outreach to the faith community. Perhaps not surprisingly, residents from the neighborhood in which FPA was least active, the SUMO area, were the most skeptical of the effort. They generally thought that faith-based organizations were being treated as a privileged group, separate from other community initiatives. The other two neighborhoods had exactly the opposite view: they held the faith community to be a vital partner. In both of these neighborhoods there were several leading pastors with a long history of partnership with public and private institutions. FPA came as a welcome and reasonable idea to them.

Interviews with leaders of faith-based organizations uncovered some common, important themes running through their perspectives on partnerships with government agencies. These themes are particularly relevant today in light of the heightened attention President Bush, federal agencies, state agencies, and foundations are giving to the public role of faith-based organizations.

*Commitment to the moral substance of their programs.* The leaders we interviewed were clear that their programs were different than secular providers in several important ways:

- Holism: They regarded their services as part of an attempt to address a person on all levels, spiritually, emotionally, physically, vocationally.
- Responsibility: They were confident in their moral authority to uphold high standards of accountability from people they serve in return for the around-the-clock compassion they offer.
- Community: They saw themselves not merely as service providers but as suppliers of a wider caring community. If a client has dental problems, for instance, then their immediate response is to connect him or her with a dentist in their congregation. They draw on other resources from within their community of faith to meet the needs of clients.

*Prudence in government partnerships.* Our interviewees showed a high degree of sophistication in their understanding of what public partnerships entail. As Goldsmith points out in Chapter Seven, faith-community leaders understand that they need to accept responsibility for reporting and all the paperwork it requires, and they understand what is and is not permissible with public funds. They also have a firm grasp on the fact that they are providing a service that must produce a public benefit.

Our interviews confirmed all of these beliefs and assumptions among pastors and directors of faith-based organizations. It is fairly common to hear the objection that faith-based organizations will become enslaved to governments, and thereby secularized, if they receive public funds. While this may be true in some places, the Indianapolis experience in general paints a picture of a group of faith-based organizations who are well-educated and wary about the promises and pitfalls of public partnerships. This, it seems, is what results from a careful and dedicated outreach to these organizations that is also sympathetic to their unique nature.

*Need for technical assistance.* People working in faith-based organizations have a fairly good understanding of what their limits are. Like any small grassroots association, they realize that public partnerships are nearly impossible without someone to help cut the red tape. FPA, which was discontinued after Goldsmith left office, is sorely missed by a number of faith leaders. They primarily miss its "civic switchboard" function, namely the manner in which it connected them to the relevant people and agencies needed to address a certain problem or create an opportunity.

They also miss the help they received finding people in the community to assist with grant writing and program oversight. They thought that if government wants to reach out to the "little guy," the grassroots group, then it needs to be prepared to help provide connections to technical assistance; otherwise, the large "usual suspects" will be the ones pulling in the large grants. Instead of simply requiring small groups to change themselves and act like a big agency, government needs to recognize their limits and use its access to information and connectivity with other organizations to supply this function if at all possible.

*Funding is only as good as the perspective you place it in.* There was a peculiar unanimity in our interviews about the value of money compared to the value of other kinds of services such as technical assistance, network-building, and red-tape cutting. Most considered these latter services as equally, if not more, important than funding. Or, funding was at least considered to be a more complicated matter if those services are found lacking. Also, large grants were viewed by some as a potential problem simply because they present a greater potential for error than, for instance, reimbursement payments (so long as they are timely).

### Endnotes

[1] For example, *Entrepreneur* ranked Indianapolis as the number-one city in the central United States for growing a business in 1999. *Inc.* magazine ranked Indianapolis as the fifth-best city in America for growing starting and expanding businesses in 1998 and 1999. Indianapolis was the only northern U.S. city to make the top ten on the list. For three straight years, *Employment Review* has named Indianapolis as one of America's best places to live and work, and *Fortune* named Indianapolis as one of the nation's most improved cities. *Nation's Cities Weekly* called it a "growth dynamo" that has set "new standards of excellence for urban renewal and economic development," and *The Christian Science Monitor* declared that Indianapolis had become a "vibrant, marquee metropolis." Because of the success of the competition program, Goldsmith was named Public Official of the Year by *Governing* magazine. Harvard Business School and the Kennedy School of Government at Harvard have made the city the subject of a number of case studies. *Financial World* named Indianapolis one of the ten best-managed cities in the nation in 1995. And the city won the Innovation in American Government Award from the Ford Foundation.

[2] Population numbers are based on the 2000 Census and are approximate. Neighborhood boundaries and census tracts do not correspond precisely, and thus a slight degree of variation must be admitted.

[3] "Historical Narrative of the Near West Side Neighborhood," The Polis Center, Indianapolis (1995): 5.

[4] "Historical Narrative of the Near West Side Neighborhood," 7-8.

[5] "A Historical Narrative of the Martindale-Brightwood Neighborhood," The Polis Center (1995): 1-2.

[6] Much of the foregoing historical background on the three neighborhoods, as is evident from the preceding footnotes, has been drawn from the excellent historical narratives prepared by The Polis Center at Indiana University-Purdue University at Indianapolis.

[7] See "Caring for Our Civic Souls," *Blue Print* 3 (Spring: 1999).

[8] Tyrone Chandler, "Reducing Gun-Related Crimes through a Comprehensive Multi-Pronged Program: The Indianapolis Weed and Seed Initiative," *Weed and Seed Best Practices* 3 (U.S. Department of Justice, Spring 2000): 10-11.

[9] Chandler, 13.

[10] I refer to their article, "Broken Windows," in 1982 in the *Atlantic Monthly*, which famously became the core thesis of the Giuliani administration's dramatically successful crime-reduction strategy, as well as Kelling's book, *Fixing Broken Windows: Restoring Order and Reducing Crime in Our Communities* (New York: Free Press, 1996).

[11] For tabulations of property and violent crimes as percentages of total crimes, see Appendix A.

[12] For a listing of the organizations in each of the neighborhoods, see Appendix C.

[13] See Robert Putnam, *Bowling Alone: The Collapse and Revival of American Community* (New York: Simon & Schuster, 2000).

[14] Community Assets, POLIS Center, 2000.

[15] Information on the number of churches by neighborhood was supplied both by the Polis Center and the Indianapolis Department of Metropolitan Development.

[16] Katherine Allen and Maria Kirby, "Unfinished Business: Why Cities Matter to Welfare Reform" (Washington, D.C.: Brookings Institution, 2000), 1, 12.

[17] For complete labor-force numbers and unemployment rates for the three neighborhoods, the city, state, and nation, see Appendix B.

[18] "Successful Business Development Projects, 1993–2000," Indianapolis Economic Development Corporation.

[19] *Federal Funds, Local Choices: An Evaluation of the CDBG Program*, vol. 1 (Washington, D.C.: HUD, 1995).

[20] Calculated from projections based on leverage estimates in the Indianapolis's Department of Metropolitan Development's CDBG Annual Reports.

[21] For a breakdown of the CDBG awards in the three neighborhoods, see the charts in Appendix C.

# Appendix A:
## Total Crimes, Crimes per 1,000 Population, and Property and Violent Crimes as a Percentage of Total Crimes[1]

Total Crimes

|  | 1993 | 1994 | 1995 | 1996 | 1997 | 1998 | 1999 |
|---|---|---|---|---|---|---|---|
| M.B. | 1,545 | 1,679 | 1,690 | 1,713 | 1,913 | 1,633 | 1,471 |
| SUMO | 2,269 | 2,510 | 2,476 | 2,541 | 3,025 | 2,752 | 2,596 |
| WESCO | 1,722 | 2,018 | 2,069 | 1,967 | 1,818 | 1,625 | 1,606 |
| CITY | 38,324 | 42,108 | 43,114 | 44,618 | 43,350 | 40,623 | 36,888 |

Crimes per 1,000 Population[2]

|  | 1993 | 1994 | 1995 | 1996 | 1997 | 1998 | 1999 |
|---|---|---|---|---|---|---|---|
| M.B. | 137 | 148 | 150 | 152 | 169 | 145 | 130 |
| SUMO | 144 | 159 | 157 | 161 | 191 | 174 | 164 |
| WESCO | 138 | 161 | 165 | 157 | 145 | 130 | 128 |
| CITY | 52 | 58 | 59 | 61 | 59 | 56 | 50 |

Property Crimes as Percentage of Total Crimes

|  | 1993 | 1994 | 1995 | 1996 | 1997 | 1998 | 1999 |
|---|---|---|---|---|---|---|---|
| M.B. | 60 | 57 | 55 | 56 | 54 | 50 | 56 |
| SUMO | 69 | 68 | 69 | 68 | 64 | 61 | 61 |
| WESCO | 69 | 69 | 65 | 60 | 59 | 53 | 54 |
| CITY | 71 | 70 | 69 | 68 | 65 | 63 | 63 |

Violent Crimes as Percentage of Total Crimes[3]

|  | 1993 | 1994 | 1995 | 1996 | 1997 | 1998 | 1999 |
|---|---|---|---|---|---|---|---|
| M.B. | 27 | 22 | 24 | 24 | 23 | 27 | 24 |
| SUMO | 15 | 14 | 12 | 14 | 15 | 17 | 18 |
| WESCO | 18 | 17 | 19 | 24 | 22 | 25 | 24 |
| CITY | 16 | 15 | 16 | 17 | 18 | 19 | 19 |

[1] Statistics in this section, other than the total crime numbers presented in the first chart, are my own analysis of aggregate numbers supplied by the Indianapolis Police Department Crime Analysis Unit, GIS.

[2] To be charitable and for the sake of constancy, the 1990 Census figures are used in these calculations. While the SUMO area's population stayed relatively constant throughout the 1990s (and, in fact, increased by more than 700 residents), the other two neighborhoods each experienced a decrease in population. Nonetheless, in the absence of exact annual numbers, the 1990s numbers are used and thus impute a charitable reading to the numbers in WESCO and Martindale-Brightwood, since lower population figures would drive the per 1,000 crime figures upward. As a whole, Indianapolis's population rose from 731,278 in the 1990 Census to 781,870 in the 2000 Census.

[3] It may be questioned at this point why the statistics in the tables above have been separated out by the percentage they represent over against the total crime number. The reason for this is simple. Neighborhood residents do not experience crime the way we often represent it in charts and tables. They do not experience aggregate numbers of murders or larceny. They experience crime, if not as a direct victim, by seeing the flashing squad-car lights, hearing gunshots, seeing broken windows and damaged building facades, listening to their neighbors complain about a missing lawnmower or deck chair, smelling smoke, hearing voices screaming or crying, and by being interrogated by police as witnesses to a crime. In a given year, when gunshots seem frighteningly numerous and police are asking lots of questions not about property crimes but drug dealers and potential murder suspects, residents feel oppressed by violence. They will want to be empowered to fight drug dealers and violent crime. It is no surprise that there is a close correlation between SUMO residents' frequent citation of property-related needs and the high percentage of property crimes in their neighborhood. They are the only neighborhood that has experienced an actual rise in violent crime, and yet the high percentage of property crimes in their neighborhood makes them feel "un-empowered" to combat what seems to be a constant threat to their property. Despite the rise in violent crime, the prevalence of property crime is what they talk about the most. And whatever residents are most concerned about is the issue around which they will organize themselves. The empowerment strategy employed by a group of residents follows their prevailing sentiments about where the problems in their community actually lie.

# Appendix B:

## Labor Force, Employed, Unemployed, and Unemployment Rate for the Three Neighborhoods, Indianapolis, Its MSA, the State of Indiana, and the Nation[1]

|  | 1992 | 1994 | 1997 | 1999 |
|---|---|---|---|---|
| **Martindale-Brightwood** | | | | |
| Labor Force | 4,875 | 5,045 | 4,875 | 4,830 |
| Employed | 4,080 | 4,370 | 4,410 | 4,430 |
| Unemployed | 795 | 675 | 360 | 400 |
| Rate | 16.3 | 13.4 | 6.5 | 5.7 |
| **SUMO** | | | | |
| Labor Force | 6,320 | 6,585 | 6,415 | 6,370 |
| Employed | 5,485 | 5,875 | 5,930 | 5,950 |
| Unemployed | 835 | 710 | 485 | 420 |
| Rate | 13.2 | 10.8 | 7.6 | 6.6 |
| **WESCO** | | | | |
| Labor Force | 5,400 | 5,645 | 5,530 | 5,500 |
| Employed | 4,780 | 5,115 | 5,170 | 5,185 |
| Unemployed | 620 | 530 | 360 | 315 |
| Rate | 11.4 | 9.4 | 6.5 | 5.7 |
| **Indianapolis** | | | | |
| Labor Force | 391,450 | 413,880 | 411,760 | 410,970 |
| Employed | 368,510 | 394,270 | 398,370 | 399,360 |
| Unemployed | 22,940 | 19,610 | 13,390 | 11,610 |
| Rate | 5.9 | 4.7 | 3.3 | 2.8 |
| **Indianapolis Metropolitan Statistical Area** | | | | |
| Labor Force | 743,100 | 800,880 | 825,440 | 833,850 |
| Employed | 703,770 | 767,800 | 802,540 | 813,660 |
| Unemployed | 39,330 | 33,080 | 22,900 | 20,190 |
| Rate | 5.3 | 4.1 | 2.8 | 2.4 |
| **Indiana** | | | | |
| Labor Force | 2,840,200 | 3,048,900 | 3,087,000 | 3,077,600 |
| Employed | 2,652,300 | 2,898,400 | 2,978,600 | 2,984,600 |
| Unemployed | 187,900 | 150,500 | 108,400 | 93,000 |
| Rate | 6.6 | 4.9 | 3.5 | 3.0 |
| **United States** | | | | |
| Labor Force | 128,105,000 | 131,056,000 | 136,297,000 | 139,368,000 |
| Employed | 118,492,000 | 123,060,000 | 129,558,000 | 133,488,000 |
| Unemployed | 9,613,000 | 7,996,000 | 6,739,000 | 5,880,000 |
| Rate | 7.5 | 6.1 | 4.9 | 4.2 |

[1] U.S. Bureau of Labor Statistics and Indiana Department of Workforce Development.

# Appendix C:
## CDBG Investment in the Three Neighborhoods, 1993-1999

Yearly CDBG Funding in the Three Neighborhoods (totals in italics)[1]

| | 1993[2] | 1994 | 1995 | 1996 | 1997 | 1998[3] | 1999 |
|---|---|---|---|---|---|---|---|
| **M.B.** | *-0-* | *12,000* | *164,000* | *290,000* | *284,000* | *66,000* | *178,000* |
| | | | | | | | |
| **Southeast** | *142,000* | *454,000* | *207,000* | *308,000* | *178,000* | *68,000* | *324,000* |
| **SEND** | -0- | 451,000 | 134,000 | 264,000 | 77,000 | 57,000 | 203,000 |
| **SUMO** | -0- | 3,000 | 73,000 | 44,000 | 101,000 | 11,000 | 121,000 |
| | | | | | | | |
| **Near West** | *90,000* | *311,000* | *422,000* | *420,000* | *430,000* | *193,000* | *517,000* |
| **West CDC** | 90,000 | 300,000 | 339,000 | 386,000 | 413,000 | 159,000 | 417,000 |
| **WESCO** | -0- | 11,000 | 83,000 | 34,000 | 17,000 | 28,000 | 100,000 |

Totals and Yearly Averages, 1993–1999

| Neighborhood | Total CDBG Receipts | Yearly Average Receipt |
|---|---|---|
| **Martindale-Brightwood** | 994,000 | 142,000 |
| **Southeast (SUMO)** | 1,681,000 | 240,000 |
| **Near West (WESCO)** | 2,383,000 | 340,000 |

Total Awarded but Not Yet Paid in Full in 1999

| Neighborhood | Total Award in 1999 |
|---|---|
| **Martindale-Brightwood** | 450,000 |
| **Southeast (SUMO)** | 476,000 |
| **Near West (WESCO)** | 662,000 |

[1] Information on CDBG disbursements has been tabulated from Indianapolis Department of Metropolitan Development's "Annual Reports on the Community Development Block Grant Program," 1993-1999. Grants to smaller, grassroots organizations are not represented in the chart, since they flowed through the umbrella organizations and are thus included in the totals to the umbrellas.

[2] In Fountain Square, the southeastern neighborhood, the $142,000 went to two organizations that merged in 1993 to form SEND, the CDC for the southeastern neighborhood.

[3] In 1998, CDBG funds began to flow even to several small grassroots organizations as well as the CDCs and umbrella associations. The grants never topped $5,000 to these small organizations, and their totals are included in the SUMO and WESCO totals for those neighborhoods and simply added to the total for Martindale-Brightwood. The most received by these small organizations in a single neighborhood was in WESCO in 1999. They account for $35,000 of the $100,000 total listed for WESCO.

# Index

# About the Author

## Stephen Goldsmith

While serving two terms as mayor of Indianapolis, Stephen Goldsmith earned a national reputation for his innovations in government. As mayor of America's twelfth-largest city, he led a nationally acclaimed effort to rebuild the capacity of the city's neglected urban neighborhoods by eliminating counterproductive regulations, reducing taxes, and leading a one-billion-dollar *Building Better Neighborhoods* campaign. The resulting transformation of downtown Indianapolis and many nearby neighborhoods brought recognition to Indianapolis as a model for urban areas throughout the nation.

Many of the efforts to revitalize Indianapolis neighborhoods involved creative partnerships with private, secular, and faith-based groups. Called the "Front Porch Alliance," the partnership became a prototype for many faith-based efforts across the country and attracted the attention of government leaders from the president to governors and other mayors.

Goldsmith is now Special Advisor to President Bush on faith-based and not-for-profit initiatives and was appointed by the President to chair the Corporation For National and Community Service. He also served as chief domestic policy advisor to the Bush presidential campaign.

He currently serves as Senior Vice President for Strategic Initiatives and e-Government for ACS Inc., Faculty Director for the Innovations in American Government program at Harvard's Kennedy School of Government, and Chairman of the Manhattan Institute's Center for Civic Innovation.

Goldsmith is a 1968 graduate of Wabash College and received his law degree from the University of Michigan in 1971. He graduated with honors and served as Associate Editor of the University of Michigan Law Review.